CAN
is the word of
POWER

❖ *A thought-provoking* ❖ *Concern-developing*
❖ *Action-initiating*
plan and work-book for the young minds!!

Barendra Kumar

UNICORN BOOKS

Publishers
UNICORN BOOKS

J-3/16 , Daryaganj, New Delhi-110002
☎ 23276539, 23272783, 23272784 • *Fax:* 011-23260518
E-mail: unicornbooks@vsnl.com
Website: www.unicornbooks.in • www.kidscorner.in

Distributors
Pustak Mahal, Delhi
Bangalore: *E-mail:* pmblr@sancharnet.in • pustak@sancharnet.in
Mumbai: *E-mail:* rapidex@bom5.vsnl.net.in
Patna: *E-mail:* rapidexptn@rediffmail.com
Hyderabad: *E-mail:* pustakmahalhyd@yahoo.co.in

• *London Office*
5, Roddell Court, Bath Road, Slough SL3 OQJ, England
E-mail: pustakmahaluk@pustakmahal.com

© **Copyright : Author**

ISBN 978-81-7806-115-3

Edition : February 2007

Printed at : Pushp Print Service, Delhi

Dedicated To

My Almighty Lord,

for His abundant grace

plus

My Late Dad, My Late Mom

who would have been happy today,

and

loving family

plus

Parents of Young Minds

who really strive hard to see them doing

better and greater.

When you are on your journey
from childhood to manhood,
here is an informational, inspirational, motivational
effort to make you a
success-conscious 'yes' thinker,
a dreamer...so also a doer.

God Bless You

Name: . . . .

Photograph

Age: . . . .

Father's Name:. . . . .

Mother's Name:. . . . .

School / College: . . . .

Address: . . . .

Tel. No.: . . . . .Mobile:. . . . .

E-mail: . . . .

Signature

Fill in the above....go through the pages.
Read, think and believe...to achieve.

Preface

The journey of a thousand miles begins with a single step. I believed in this Chinese proverb when I thought of preparing a book. My effort gradually gained momentum, till you have it in your hand. As a human being on Earth, I thank God and as an Indian I feel proud of sharing my thoughts, my experiences, my knowledge with the help of a few words, to elevate your feelings for a better life and a better nation.

Most of the time I wondered and questioned myself about my life, others' life, and developed a curiosity to know the secret of living. I thought about what responsibility we owe, what we should do, what we can do as human beings, as citizens of a great country. The answers I found led to the formation of this book, for all **the young minds of our nation.**

We have enough reasons to feel proud of our nation, our rich heritage and glorious past, still there are areas that really need everybody's attention and concern. **The strength of a nation depends on the individuals and the hope lies with the young minds.** When I thought a little more, I was delighted to find one thing common in almost all the elders, that irrespective of position and occupation, all are concerned to have a better child, better young mind, better nation. Moreover, most of us agree in one aspect – that we need to improve, need to advance, need to excel – and that can be possible only with inventive and creative thoughts, ideas and efforts, taken by **the young minds who are in millions, and are the greatest natural resource with potential power, capable to perform excellently to build a better and greater nation.** *We have experienced that a single invention creates wealth and employment for millions, a single discovery helps eradicating diseases, a single creative thought and act* *empowers and prospers a nation, even changes the face of the world.* Undoubtedly, as elders, we make great efforts to nourish and teach, shape and mould the young minds, performing the best, but a little more information, a little more inspiration, a little more motivation will surely help them to think a little more, believe a little more, and act a little more, *when united can achieve much more.*

Thus, this book is prepared for the young minds like you, to think and harness your power within you, act and take help from the people around you, plan and use the time ahead of you.

— It is **informational**, because it contains information about your personal development and growth – *spiritual, mental, emotional and physical.*

— It is **inspirational**, because it allows you to come across the *great thoughts, great quotes of great people* to be inspired.

— It is **motivational**, because it *induces you to think and act,* look and find, know and discover, learn and earn, believe and achieve to build a better you, yield a greater you. It can console you, it can guide you, it can support you, it can encourage you, it can educate you, it can inform you, it can inspire you, it can motivate you – when you read it, reread it, believe in it and act according to it.

This is prepared and meant for all the young minds, whether he or she, though, throughout the book the gender is he/him. This is a book you can consider for self-success, self-improvement, self-analysis with special emphasis on **creative, inventive thoughts, ideas for peace, progress and prosperity of you, your family, your community and your nation.**

- Pre-read the book.
- Read the book, carefully, think ..... and read .... read and think .... till you finish.

- Read the book, start using it as your personal work book, find and note down, fill and feel, grow and glow to believe and act on your part. Don't expect a great change instantly, because change is a process and a matter of patience. It is essential that you get ready for a change. I have a few words, nothing new, for **the parents and teachers**, who are directly responsible for you, whom I request to read, think and do a little more for you, to fulfil a noble objective for a greater nation. I adapt the quote of **the great thinker-poet Johann Wolfgang Von Goethe** and request you to read, man/young mind:

"Treat a man/young mind as he appears to be and you make him worse, but treat a man/young mind as if he already were what he potentially could be and you make him what he should be."

We treat you, as you potentially could be.... and expect the best from you. Develop your skill, your talent and go ahead to live *a life—meaningful, useful, resourceful for self and society*. Train your life to move forward, upward, Godward and start to act.... with all your heart...

You can have more of you!

You can build a better you!

You can yield a greater you!

CAN IS THE WORD OF POWER!

—**Barendra Kumar**

Acknowledgements

*F*irst of all, I thank and praise God for His abundant grace to complete this book. I have my heartfelt gratitude for the people, who have succeeded in their lives to inspire not only me but all the readers, by their great achievements and accomplishments in different areas of life, for the progress of human race.

I humbly respect and salute the great philosophers, thinkers, scientists, psychologists, reformers, statesmen, for their valuable effort, contribution to make the world a little better. I am really indebted to those great people who have lived and are living with a great concern for the betterment of our nation.

This book is a result of my thoughts and efforts for years, based on my experiences and knowledge I gained throughout my life at different times, different places and from different sources, the original works sometimes neither mentioned, nor exactly and flawlessly traceable. Regardless of the source, I thank and express my gratitude to all the people for their efforts to disseminate knowledge on this planet Earth.

My efforts to prepare this could be possible with the help of many people around me for years. To mention, first, my mother, who stood as a physical being when I started but remains to stand as an all-time inspiration, spiritually. My brothers, sisters, uncles, aunts, cousins, in-laws, wife, loving son, friends, relatives, colleagues, authorities who were always behind me to encourage, support and guide. Parents, teachers, common citizens have always helped by giving their views, comments, suggestions, constructive criticism during my experimentation and preparation. Young minds belonging to various age groups, from various places and varieties of background, known and unknown have inspired, nay, induced me to hold the pen for them and strive hard for years to complete the same. I thank and pray for all.

I am very much thankful to Dr. Ashok Gupta of Unicorn Books and his supporting team for their active cooperation at every step in bringing out this book in its present form.

In the end, with utmost humility I apologise for any inadvertent omission and invite suggestions and comments for correction and rectification in the further editions, with a higher sense of gratitude to everyone, who has contributed to this publication for the improvement, betterment, advancement of **the young minds, the future of our nation**.

—**Barendra Kumar**
E-Mail: canisthewordofpower@gmail.com

Contents

৯০ ୭ଷ

YOU
CAN HAVE
MORE OF YOU

Man often becomes what
he believes himself to be. If I keep
on saying to myself that I cannot do
a certain thing, it is possible that
I may end by really becoming
incapable of doing it. On the contrary,
if I have the belief that I can do it,
I shall surely acquire the capacity to do it,
even if I may not have it at the beginning.

—*Mahatma Gandhi*
The Father of Nation

The great visionary, with his magnetic personality, had really understood, experienced, exhibited the power of belief and truth in his life. He expressed goodwill and fine feelings for the countrymen, avoided guns and violence, united millions of people and went against all odds for years and achieved freedom for you and me. He strived hard to make INDIA attain a great name in the history of the world, and also lived a life to influence, inspire, encourage the vast majority of the Indian masses.....for centuries.

After more than half a century of our freedom, as a young mind of India, can you think, realise, understand what we have achieved and what not? What we can achieve and how? And can you decide to apply the power of belief in your life to build a better and greater **YOU** by achieving a worthy goal, for a **better and greater nation?**

CAN is the Word of Power

Did is a word of Achievement,
Won't is a word of Retreat,
Might is a word of Bereavement,
Can't is a word of Defeat,
Ought is a word of Duty,
Try is a word of the Hour,
Will is a word of Beauty,
Can is a word of Power.

—Anonymous

*Y*ES...

CAN IS THE WORD OF POWER!

CAN'T IS NOT, IT IS OF DEFEAT!!

Can is a magic word. It has the power to do anything.... do everything. It changes things, changes people, changes places. It helps in inventions, in discoveries, in progress, in advancements. It removes obstructions, strikes hindrances, dilutes barriers. It changes seemingly impossible into possible. It changes poverty into riches. It changes weak into healthy. It changes miserable into joyful. It develops courage, gives strength, builds conviction, induces action for a great cause, and helps to achieve your goal.

Can programs your mind, Can makes you believe,

to accomplish.... to achieve....

Mahatma Gandhi brought freedom for India,

Edison invented the electric bulb,

Fleming discovered Pencillin,

What do you think helps you dare – having sufficient opportunities or having the power of can? Yes, CAN helps you to dare to THINK...Think that you can. Believe that you can. Act as if you can....Do something good, something great, for yourself, for your family, for your community, for your country...for the world...

When you think and accept strongly, you empower your belief, which changes your feelings and consequently your response. Obviously, when response changes, your effort changes and thus.....your result.....your goal.....your destiny.

Look at yourself, the clothes you wear, the bike you ride, the television you watch, the cellular phone you talk into...could be possible...because the people behind them thought they CAN.

The industries, the businesses, the entrepreneurship, the medicines, the pacemaker, the kidney transplantation... could be possible because somebody thought he CAN.

From wheel to abacus, from printing press to rockets, from microscope to submarine, from photography to telegraph, from synthetic fibre to audiotape, from fax to video, from laser to computer...could be made available.....

The Pyramids of Egypt ....The Great Wall of China.... The magnificent Taj Mahal could be possible.....

Because somebody strived hard, some people tried hard, believing that they can... so THEY COULD.

The power of belief helped **Vasco Da Gama** to see the land, beyond the sea,

It helped **Henry Ford** to put people on wheels,

It helped **Nelson Mandela** to abolish apartheid.

Believe in the Power of Can.......

Believe in the power of belief.

It can energise you to live a life....to the fullest,

yes, a life...not merely an existence.

> *We live in a marvellous age;*
> *Live in it!*
> *Too many of us just exist in it.*
> —*Martin Panzer*

Live for a successful career, a meaningful life. Don't live a life as because you have no reason to die. Believe to improve in studies, to better in career and yield greater in life. Don't believe in those people who do not believe in the power of belief. Their favourite word is **can't**. The people in favour of can't do not find anything good, do not feel anything good, do not do anything good. They blame others, blame circumstances, blame their inactivities. They do not dare to believe and do not try to make something happen to them. They do not dare even to wish... to do something.

They know that Man has landed on the moon,

they know that Man has invented the computer,

they know that there are achievements and achievers...

they know that they are also human beings...

Still, when it comes to them, they dare not. They feel and utter... **can't. They are for defeat.** But, **you can,** you all can do miracles, can do wonders because the future belongs to you. Be a lover of **CAN**. Can will surely give the courage to lift your score. Can will surely make you determined to brighten your career. Can will surely fill you with power to procure happiness, for more and more.

Fill your mind with the power of CAN. Let it go into your mind and flow through your body. Let it show for others...

Live a meaningful life by achieving a worthy cause, a valuable goal. Do what is necessary, learn what is necessary. **Develop yourself, imagine great, dream big, aim high, think success, see progress.** You have a brain in your head and you can have a choice in your brain. Decide and go ahead, believing that YOU CAN...

If you persuade yourself that you can do a certain thing, you will do it, however difficult it may be. If, on the contrary, you imagine that you can't do the simplest thing in this world, it is impossible for you to do, and molehills become for you unscalable mountains.

—*Emile Coue*

The 'time' is for you, hold it, hug it. Find a place for yourself, in this universe. Build a life to give a life message. Show your family what you can accomplish! Show your community what your potential is! Show your nation who are you going to be! *Make your life a masterpiece.* Develop the will and the skill. Take the responsibility and have a turning point in your life. Be sure, your conscious and consistent efforts will make everything possible. At the same time, let us not forget that there is no magic seed, which grows and yields fruit in one day. So to start...is to start with 'Can'. Get ready to get along with CAN and never with can't.

Can't seizes you	— CAN moves you.
Can't declares 'impossible'	— CAN finds 'may be possible'.
Can't shows arrogance	— CAN shows humility.
Can't observes dead end	— CAN looks at new beginning.
Can't refutes	— CAN regains.
Can't broods on 'What I don't have'	— CAN gathers 'Whatever I have'.
Can't utters 'excuses'	— CAN takes 'responsibilities'.
Can't behaves 'I know much'	— CAN steps out, to learn much.
Can't is rude and stubborn	— CAN is caring and kind.
Can't creates conflicts	— CAN settles contrasts.
Can't is for frustration	— CAN is for solution.
Can't abuses one and all	— CAN respects one and all.
Can't makes fun of others	— CAN makes fun for others.
Can't retaliates	— CAN reconciles.
Can't criticises	— CAN advises.
Can't ridicules	— CAN encourages.
Can't avoids a job	— CAN welcomes a job.
Can't defends a fault	— CAN repents for a fault.

Can't favours confusions	— CAN favours convictions.
Can't builds complaints	— CAN makes compliments.
Can't focusses on weakness	— CAN focusses on strength.
Can't folds the arm	— CAN moves forward.
Can't cries on pain	— CAN tolerates for a gain.
Can't stops	— CAN starts.
Can't steals the power	— **CAN fills you with POWER**.

Until you try, you don't know
what you can't do.

—*Henry James*

ॐ ℃ॐ

CAN
is a
Decision

The future belongs to those,
who learn what they need to learn,
in order to do what they need to do.
                                        —*Denis Waitley*

*H*ow can you do better in studies? How can you excel in your career?

How can you be successful in your life? How can you be happy?

How can you be rich? How can you be a better human being?

How can you get – what you really want to get out of your life?

The answer is – **by decision... then action.**

Learn to decide .... before you decide to learn...

When you decide, you take responsibility, take control, take charge of your life. You understand in which direction you are headed towards. Through indecision, your career is ruined, opportunities are lost and life may seem – broken. Then – you have to accept, you have to take for granted, you have to be content with what life brings to you. So decide now. What you want? What you can? How you can?

DECIDE NOW – DO YOU BELIEVE IN THE POWER OF CAN?

Your future depends on the decision you make today, and the action you take today.

Learn to think.... Learn to decide.... Learn to act.

You should or shouldn't? Can or can't?.... Even if CAN, then WHY?.... **NOW!!!**

Because, it is a matter of **your life**. You must have heard life is a journey. Then – what is the destination? To put it simply, life is a period. By that we understand it as a combination of some years, which are a combination of some months, which in reality are a combination of some days, then hours, minutes, seconds. If you lose some seconds, some minutes, some hours, some days, some months or years – **you lose it out of your life** – through **indecision**.

> *Time marches by*
> *the months, the years, they fly,*
> *it runs out for some,*
> *for others it is just begun.*
>
> —*Anonymous*

All the treasures on Earth can't bring back a single lost second, a single lost minute. Life is precious. So also is TIME. It can't be purchased, borrowed, hoarded. It can only be spent, invested – wisely or unwisely. So why to waste something you can't recapture.

God has blessed everyone with the same twenty-four hours in a day. Everyone living on Earth spends it. One reaches the sky, another looks at it. One climbs the mountain – another, the staircase. One earns crores – another mere hundreds. Everyone is busy, everyone seems to be busy. Is that enough? Busy – but for WHAT? Account every second. Consider every minute – don't lose even a little of it. Little is not big, but little makes big.

Little fun, little relaxation, but not little indecision....

Be careful about your time. You will suffer, if you lose it. You will repent, if you abuse it. You will feel happy, feel better, feel great – if you USE it. USE it now. Decide now....

– Believe in God – expect great blessings.

– Believe in your parents – expect great support.

– Believe in your teachers, counsellors – expect great guidance.

What more do you want?

The whole world is not there, when you decide,

But the whole world is with you – when you succeed.

> *The future belongs to those*
> *who fuse intelligence*
> *with faith and who with courage*
> *and determination grope their way forward*
> *from chance to choice,*
> *from blind adaptation to creative evolution.*
> —*Charles E. Merriam*

ℰ ☙

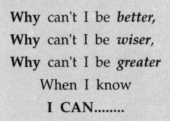

Why can't I be *better,*
Why can't I be *wiser,*
Why can't I be *greater*
When I know
I CAN........

CAN IS THE WORD
OF
POWER

Do all the good you can
By all the means you can
In all the ways you can
At all the times you can
To all the people you can
As long as ever you can.

—*John Wesley*

CAN for a Successful Career, Meaningful Life

It is no use saying "We are doing our best".
You have got to succeed in doing
what is necessary.
—Winston Churchill

Life – for most of the people, is monotonous, dull, even painful – except a few, whose life seems exciting, bright and joyful. Most of the people are busy with their daily chores, daily trifles – except a few, those think and do something worthwhile. Most of the people blame on situations, on circumstances – except a few, who strive for a solution.

Is life full of barriers and battlements only? Is life full of hurdles and obstacles only? Is life full of misery and confusion only?

How do some people live a different life? A life of hope and expectation, a life of joy and happiness, a life of achievements and accomplishments, a life of fulfilment, a life of success.

Nothing happens by chance.

So also is the case with Success!

There is a reason for everything. For every effect there is a cause. The revolution of Earth, the sprouting of a seed, the blowing of wind holds a reason within – whether we know or not, whether we realise or not, whether we accept or not.

For many people, money determines success. If one has sufficient money, he is successful...Right.... Maybe..?

Money is the result, the outcome of success. If one has enough money, essentially he is not successful but if one is successful, he can have as much as he needs.

> *The energetic men who make great fortunes*
> *seldom desire the actual money.*
> *They desire the sense of power through*
> *a contest and the joy of successful activity.*
> —*Bertrand Russell*

A successful leader changes the course of a nation, for better,

A successful scientist changes the history of science, for better,

A successful industrialist changes the fate of an industry, for better,

A successful doctor changes the condition of a fellow human being, for better,

A successful architect changes the set-up of a location, for better.

A successful teacher changes the career and life of a student, for better.

A successful student changes himself – to grow, to be a good citizen, to change the **future of a nation** – for better.

Successful people may or may not have money – but they live their life to the fullest. They enjoy their work – and fight the battle of life happily. They live for themselves and for others. They live for a worthy goal.

Success does not necessarily mean that we must earn a great deal of money and live in the biggest house in the town. It only means that we are engaged in striving towards a goal that we have independently chosen, and feel it is worthy of us as persons. A goal, whatever it may be, is what gives meaning to our existence.

—Earl Nightingale

The people who decide to be successful believe in the power of CAN. They believe and create the ability within themselves. They try to be the best and try to do the best – by excelling themselves for better and better – in any field they work, in any surrounding they serve, in any sphere they perform. They are happy people, relaxed people, contented people. They do the right and never feel to do the wrong. They hold their integrity firm and are never discouraged. They solve the problems of life with a smile. They put their effort for public need, and use their power and energy for the people around. They inspire others, motivate others to labour better. They are the achievers in their mini universe.

Out of them, some people achieve more than that...

They think of themselves...and a few more people...

They think of themselves...and a far more people...

They think of themselves.... and a great more people...

They find the need of all. They solve the problems of all. They think the life of all. They are total success.

Total success is the continuing involvement in the pursuit of a worthy ideal, which is being realised for the benefit of others – rather than at their expense.

—Denis Waitley

Their life is total success, great success, which makes them great.

Greatness lies in their efforts, in their achievements to fulfil a worthy goal – for the benefit of others, for the welfare of others, for the betterment of others.

They are great dreamers! Great achievers!

They think success. They imagine success. They dream success.They are conscious – to be successful. Every step they take, they make it sure they are nearer to the worthy goal.

They believe they can and that helps them to rise above the circumstances.

They believe they can and that helps them to plan and start.

They believe they can and that helps them to keep on sticking to their work......

Till they achieve, till they are successful.

They realise the purpose of life no sooner they come across the facts and tacts of living. They think of life for themselves, for others. They are thinkers and achievers.

They are positive thinkers...possibility thinkers... productive thinkers.. They believe in themselves and believe in God – and not in circumstances.

*⨍ People are always blaming their circumstances
for what they are. I don't believe in circumstances.
The people who get on in this world are the people
who get up and look for the circumstances they want,
and if they can't find them, make them.*
                                    —*George B. Shaw*

Rising above the circumstances, they start a life.

A life of hope, a life of expectation, a life of promise.

They keep interest, desire and vision for – tomorrow. For them, life is a chance. They take the chance. They dare and they do. They believe in the power of universe and the power of their mind. They concentrate on their objective and harness their power. They have definite plan, definite purpose, definite goal in life. They set the goal and seize the opportunity. They plan, they work. They are decisive, determined, dedicated. They are committed, disciplined, persistent. They stand on their convictions and fight for their principles. They believe in hard work and continuous effort, and are never influenced by remarks and opinions of others. They work on their shortcomings, their failings – improve and increase enough strength to face the hurdles and hassles. They acquire and nurture faith and grow in patience. They put the whole effort and try long enough, hard enough – even changing the stumbling blocks into stepping stones. They learn from everything they experience and train themselves to go through the disappointments. They take the sufferings as blessings and strive hard and surmount them. They never accept defeat but continue to move forward against all odds. They expand, they create, they improve. They innovate, they invent, they discover. They make good things happen, useful things happen, astonishing things happen. They are leaders, innovators, trendsetters. They direct, control, guide the events of history – and the life of human race.

> *The heights great men reached and kept*
> *were not attained by sudden flight,*
> *but, they while their companions slept,*
> *were toiling upwards in the night.*
> —*Henry W. Longfellow*

On the other hand, there are some people who wish success, but think failure. They rearrange the facts and information of failure in their mind and can't dare to do anything. They desire success – but imagine obstacles, visualise hindrances, estimate hurdles. They find reasons, they blame circumstances, they make excuses. They have enough information on how things can't be achieved. They have enough examples of how many people have failed. They have enough justification **why and how they can't do.** Their mind is filled with enough failure stories. They believe in God, but not in His power. They believe in themselves but never harness their power. They are crippled with diffidence. They are afraid to dream, hesitant to start, reluctant to work – wholeheartedly. They are indecisive and confused. They are irresolute and lack determination, commitment, conviction. They waste their time, money and energy without a definite purpose. They never try to improve their knowledge and never sharpen their intelligence. When they come across the sufferings, the pains, the troubles, they accept the temporary defeat as failure. They leave their dream midway, not realising that the next step would have led them to success. They never persist, but declare impossible...**I Can't**...

They compromise with life, adjust with situations... remain mediocre... with aspirations inside, motives buried and dreams unfinished.

They remain success wishers, but failure achievers.

Some out of them fill themselves with confusion, misery, unhappiness, discouragement and frustration. Their excitement for life disappears, and they live a stressful, depressed life.

They accept themselves as failures – until they realise their power to turn it into success. Some also move away from values, from ethics and fail in personal life, in professional life, in social life.

Failure is a good teacher – or a bad pupil. Failure teaches – how not to fail. Failure can be turned into success if it is accepted as a teacher, if it is taken as a turning point, if it is taken as a new beginning to nurture new hope, new faith, new possibility, new promise for life.

Failure teaches	—	One to admit "I'm sorry" and ask for help.
Failure teaches	—	One to have faith in God to come out of disillusionment, disappointment.
Failure teaches	—	One to reprogram the mind, renew the strength.
Failure teaches	—	One to plan being in misery, in confusion, even.
Failure teaches	—	One to start afresh with whatever is left.
Failure teaches	—	One to grow even being reproved, even being criticised.
Failure teaches	—	One to persevere till he succeeds.

There, failure becomes the pillar of success. Have you ever come across failure, or those who have failed in exam, in career, in life? Some of them are discouraged people. They are crushed, defeated, fatigued.

They may be your relative, your mate, your friend, may be ANYONE.

It is easy to make fun of them...

It is easier to advise them...

It is easiest to criticise them...

But is it really required?

As a fellow human being, encourage them. Your little word of praise, little warm smile, a little encouragement – may help them to stand on their feet for a better tomorrow, believing that – "All things....all things....their failure too shall pass away", and by doing so, you too shall be blessed.

> *Failure is the only opportunity to begin again,*
> *more intelligently.*
>
> *—Henry Ford*

If you have ever failed or you have never... it does not matter. Anyone can be successful... anyone can think success....

You too can be successful!

You too can be total success!

You too can be great success!

Think that you can. Believe that you can – you are the *Wonderful Creation of God.* You have the same inborn God-given potentiality. You can have the same universal power to work for you. Harness it – direct it towards your worthy goal.

> *The man who succeeds above his fellows is the one*
> *who early in life clearly discerns his object, and*
> *towards that object habitually directs his powers.*
> —*Lord Edward George Bulwer-Lytton*

Command your mind. Suggest your mind. Program your mind. Your subconscious mind will accept it and will guide you to achieve your goal. Don't think of your past. Your present decides your future. Be concerned, make use of your present.

> *If one would be successful in the future,*
> *let him make the most of the present.*
> —*Mary Baker Eddy*

Think Success! Talk Success! Visualise Success!

Let not the circumstances frighten you – they are the rulers of the weak. Let not the trifles disturb you – life is too precious to spend on it. Let not others pull you – it is not the pull of gravity. Stop worrying, stop moaning, stop groaning, stop complaining – start thinking. Your thought will create your future. Give up laziness. Develop courage. Build conviction. Add knowledge. Increase efficiency.

> *It is more than probable that the*
> *average individual without any injury to health,*
> *can increase his efficiency 50%.*
> —*Walter Dill Scott*

Concentrate fully. Attempt thoroughly. Proceed positively. Your brain has enough power – capable of storing enough information, manipulating enough facts, producing the best.

Don't be astonished to know – Every cubic inch of your three-pound brain contains atleast a hundred million nerve cells – interconnected by ten thousand miles of fibres – the complex power producing plant given to us by GOD.

Can you realise the performance and power of a computer – a human invention? *Yes, your brain is much more powerful than the most powerful computer of the world –* believe in your brain.

Use it More .... Make it Better.....

Be decisive, be devoted, be committed – to tackle boldly the heavy odds and move forward – on the path of success. Put your cent percent energy, cent percent ability, cent percent effort – to achieve a worthy goal.

If we did all the things we are capable of doing,
we would literally astonish ourselves.
—Thomas A. Edison

POWER! ENERGY! ABILITY!

Knowledge – can be accumulated,

Experience – can be gained,

Result – can be produced,

if the desire, if the decision, if the purpose is strong.

Accumulate, experience.

Depend on the knowledge industry....

To learn, to know, to gain, to go, towards your goal.

With knowledge – you can take a risk.

With skill – you can start a work.

With experience – you can perform a task.

Books, Periodicals, Newspapers, Television, Internet, Libraries.

Knowledge first – pleasure next,

Action first – fun next,

Goal first – trivials next.

Be fully attentive.... Fully alert.... Fully awake.

> *Compared to what we ought to be*
> *we are only half awake.*
> *We are making use of only a small part of*
> *our physical and mental resources.*
> —*William James*

You have enough power within you – harness it,

you have enough people around you – take help,

you have enough time ahead of you – use it,

you have enough knowledge nearby you – gain it.....

Believe that you CAN!

Can is the word of power.

Can't... is of defeat.

You are not born great.......

You are not from a great family........

You do not have enough education.......

You do not have enough support.......

You do not have enough capital.......

You do not have enough opportunity......
You do not have enough knowledge......

> *Be not afraid of greatness,*
> *some are born great,*
> *some achieve greatness,*
> *and some have greatness thrust upon them.*
> **—William Shakespeare**

If you are born great, then congratulations!

If you are not, even then you can do something worthy, something exemplary, something GREAT.

- **Mahatma Gandhi**, the great 'Father of the Nation' – came from a merchant family – united millions of people, struggled hard and made India free.

- **George Washington** – the President of USA – was the son of a farmer.

- **Abraham Lincoln** – the President of USA – was the son of a carpenter, was self taught. He failed in different spheres for years. Yet he persisted – finally succeeded.

- **Calvin Coolidge** – the President of USA – was the son of a storekeeper.

- **Harry S. Truman** – the President of USA – was the son of a farmer. He never attended college, failed in business – finally succeeded.

- **Zail Singh** – the President of India – came from a simple family.

- **President A.P.J. Abdul Kalam** – came from a middle class family.

- **Dhirubhai Ambani** – the dreamer industrialist, founder of Reliance Industries was not born great, but could achieve great dreams.

- **G.D.Birla** – the great industrialist, came from a remote village, in the dry region of Rajasthan, had little education. Today, Birla Industries provides textile, cement, sugar, paper, cycles...

- **Christopher Columbus** – the great navigator and explorer, was the son of a poor weaver.

- **William Shakespeare** – whose literature dominates for more than four centuries, was the son of a glovemaker. Shakespeare is the most popular author among film makers. There have been almost three hundred film productions of his major plays.

- **Charles Dickens** – the great novelist was born as the son of a humble newspaper reporter. Because of debt, his father was thrown into jail. He was very poor, and was working in a rat-infested warehouse. His job was to paste the labels on bottles. Later grew to be a great novelist.

- **Napoleon Hill** – the great author often termed as 'Father of Success' was born into a poor family, in rural Virginia. He was orphaned at the age of twelve – later developed to be one of the great authors, to come up with a success formula to make wealth.

- **Dale Carnegie** – came from a poor family, his father could not afford the expense at college. With only one good suit, he developed himself, later to write, *"How to stop worrying and start living"*, *"How to win friends and influence people"*......

- **Michael Faraday** – the physicist, discoverer of electric and magneto-electric induction, was the son of a bookbinder.

- **James Watt** – the inventor of the steam engine, was the son of an ordinary bookmaker.

- **Thomas Alva Edison** – the inventor of electric light bulb, phonograph, and motion pictures, had little schooling. He failed 10,000 times before he invented the electric bulb!

- **The Wright brothers** – didn't attend college but with effort and determination, they could make – the airplane.

- **Henry Ford** – didn't have much education – but, could produce automobiles (Ford Motor Company) for all, and grew to be the wealthiest man.

- **Aesop** – the great story writer was a Phrygian slave with deformed physique – famous for the most popular stories *"Aesop's Fables"*.

- **Demosthenes** – was initially stammering in his speech. But later he grew to be a great orator.

- **Benjamin Disraeli** – the great orator of England, was also laughed at in his first attempt but later – people listened to him attentively.

- **Ralph Waldo Emerson** – the great American philosopher's first book took very long time to be sold. Today his writing, his thought, gives knowledge to millions and millions of people all over the world.

- Great authors – **Harriet Beecher** (*Uncle Tom's Cabin*), **Dante** (*Divine Comedy*) and great poets like **William Wordsworth, Samuel Taylor Coleridge,**

John Keats – came and produced outstanding literary performances – in spite of being in poverty.

- **Mahatma Gandhi** – wrote a major portion of his autobiography *"My Experiments With Truth"* when he was in Yervada jail in Pune.

- **Jawaharlal Nehru** – wrote his famous books *"Letters From A Father To His Daughter"*, *"Glimpses of World History"*, *"Discovery of India"* – when he was imprisoned in different jails of India.

- **Henry David Thoreau** – the great author was a school teacher and a pencil maker.

- **O' Henry (William Sidney Porter)** – the great short story writer, wrote many of his short stories – while he was imprisoned for five years.

- **Napoleon Bonaparte** – had skin diseases all through his life – but that did not prevent him from being a great military and political leader.

- **Julius Caesar** – Roman statesman, had fits.

- **Ludwig Van Beethoven** – the great German composer and pianist was deaf.

- **Samuel Johnson** – the English writer known for *"A Dictionary of the English Language"* had scrofula – a disease with swelling in glands.

- **John Milton** – the great English poet (*"Paradise Lost"*) was blind.

- **Surdas** (Hindi), **Bhima Bhoi** (Oriya) – both poets, were blind.

- **Helen Keller** – blind and deaf since early childhood, became a world famous writer and public speaker.

- **Franklin Roosevelt** – was crippled by polio, but was not defeated, and achieved well, being the President of USA.
- **Sean Connery** – the great actor (James Bond) was a bricklayer and truck driver – in his early days.
- **Elvis Presley** – the singer, was once a truck driver.
- **Oprah Winfrey** – not thin, not glamorous, but could be a powerful host on TV.
- **Tenzing Norgay** – a Sherpa tribe (porter), could be with Edmund Hillary and became the first in India to climb the Mount Everest (8,848 m.), was born in poverty and want.
- **Les Brown, Anthony Robbins** – authors and motivators, were not rich when they started their career.
- **Claude M. Bristol** – an author and motivational speaker, was a newspaper man who started from the bottom to reach the top.
- **Kalpana Chawla** – although being an Indian woman – could make it great as an astronaut.
- **Meghnad Saha** – the great Indian scientist, was once helped by a doctor to pursue his studies.
- **Ramanujam** – had to undergo great financial hardships, and was initially appointed as a clerk – later grew to be a world renowned mathematician.
- **Reader's Digest** – the most popular magazine throughout the world, was started with a borrowed capital of US $1300.
- **Dave Thomas** – founder of Wendy's Restaurant, was a high school drop-out and poor. Today, there

are thousands of restaurants all over the world – to his credit.

- **Rai Bahadur M.S. Oberoi** – was poor – who later grew to be the wealthiest man having Oberoi Group of hotels all over the world.

- **Sahara India Parivar** – started with very little capital but grew to be great.

- **Narayana Murthy's Infosys** – the great software company was started with a seed capital of $250.

- **Azim Premji** – built a great software empire WIPRO – converting his tradional business of oil mill.

- A great actor like **Amitabh Bachchan** – had also faced setbacks – but he bounced back, with amazing power.

- Today, Indian Cricketers are a great success!

- Indian Tennis stars are a great success!

- **Maneka Gandhi** – for environment, **Prof M.S Swaminathan** – for Green Revolution are great successes.

- Indian author, motivator **Shiv Khera** – is a great success.

- Indians have great potential – in the field of software, in the field of management.

- Indians are the most prosperous immigrant community in USA.

- In every field, there are Indians – who are great successes.

- Indian talent is superb......You are Indian......
  You are talented......

Follow success! Imagine success! Dream success!

Our history is full of such stories telling us about the great leaders, great freedom fighters, great scientists, great industrialists, great achievers in different fields. Even today, you can find a lot many people who try long enough and hard enough.... to achieve a worthy goal, proving themselves as innovators, trendsetters........

Be conscious, gather success information, search for success principles – achieve success!

You will find not less, but more. A lot more....

YOU TOO CAN BE SUCCESSFUL!!!

Everyone has inside of him a piece of good news.
The good news is that you really don't know,
how great you can be,
how much you can love,
what you can accomplish,
what your potential is!

—*Anne Frank*

You can do it for yourself

1. Name some more people who are successful.

In the World:

_____

_____

_____

In India:

_____

_____

_____

In your City/Town/Area:

_____

_____

_____

2. Are you a success thinker?

_____

_____

3. Do you think you too can be successful?

_____

ॐ ॐ

CAN for Better Education, Better Knowledge

It is absurd to sow little but weeds in the first half of one's life time and to expect to harvest a valuable crop in the second half.
—*Percy Johnston*

The first part of life, be it half, or one third, or so, is spent on EDUCATION, on acquisition of knowledge, which is generally used to make a living or a livelihood. The first part goes in sowing, to be reaped in the next. What you sow, how well you sow, ultimately decides what you reap and how well you reap. Thus, education is vital for your life. But what does education really mean? How should and how can you be educated depends on you, as much as on your educators.

Does education mean roting or storing some information, some fact for the purpose of answering examination to pass through, in order to get diplomas, degrees, certificates only **or** to aquire, accumulate, absorb knowledge to make it useful for your life?

That education is of value which draws out the
faculties of a student so as to enable him or her
solve correctly the problems of life in every department.
                                                    —*Mahatma Gandhi*

Education doesn't end with textbooks, rather it starts with them. Reading dozens of books on environment, on pollution, but never bothering to plant a seedling in a lifetime – can this be termed as education? Storing hundreds of scientific laws but never wondering to make use of it for human need – can it be called education? Enjoying all the national holidays in the name of our national heroes, but never aspiring to spend some moments on reading, learning, knowing them, their efforts – is it real education?

If you think, if you desire, if you are determined, you can have better education, of greater value, which can help you to realise and act, build and create, increase and produce the capacity to differentiate – good and bad, sweet and bitter, clean and unclean thoughts and deeds. You can master how to behave and how to believe, how to decide and how to act, how to learn and how to earn. You can have the courage and determination to dissipate your fears, overcome your anxiety and remove your worry and to grow to be a man – useful, resourceful and beneficial for self and society. You can cultivate individual integrity, which can collectively form a good ethical environment, establishing harmony between you and the society, when you decide so.

The principle of education is to create men
who are capable of doing new things,
not simply repeating what generations have done—
Men, who are creative, inventive urd discoverers.
                                                    —*Jean Piaget*

To learn to love, to learn to be honest, to learn to be kind – being empathetic, concerned and sensitive – is a part of education.

When faith in God is doubted, the value of ethics is eroded and idleness is practised, national strength – the human resource – is depleted, and degenerated. **To think big, to aim high** is essential, along with the textbook education – to be useful to eradicate human confusion, human misery and human diseases. Prejudices, evil acts stand as barriers, obstacles, roadblocks because of ignorance. The true guiding path is education, which can ensure better and greater benefits by inventions, discoveries and implementing greater ideas to provide peace, progress and prosperity to one and all. When knowledge is disseminated and faith is asserted – greater, compelling, powerful ideas become available, worth millions and billions for millions and billions.

Therefore education stands for knowledge and knowledge becomes power – because it is put to use, and put to use for people, for nation.

You can widen your horizon and develop your vision for common beings. You can grow in wisdom, in understanding, in judgement and can equip yourself to meet the challenges of age – developing your ability to meet the consistent problems of society or nation with your intelligent solution, knowing, tapping, using the universal power of God.

You can gain abundant knowledge from the storehouse of books, where the results and experiences of great people are stored.

You can develop courage, commitment, conviction, to increase your standard of intelligence and enhance your intellectual base. Keeping in mind individual financial benefit, you can also strive hard to be educated with morality and purity, and work for the nation to prosper.

The prosperity of a country depends not in the abundance of its revenues, nor in the strength of its fortification, nor in the beauty of its public buildings, but it consists in the number of its cultivated citizens, in its men of education, enlightenment and character.
                              —*Martin Luther King Jr.*

Practical application of scientific knowledge can be developed by reconsidering, reflecting, researching the information, the fact, the data of yesteryears and by viewing various objects of Nature and universe, to use the natural resources for national wealth. Result-oriented technical knowledge can be expanded by opening the mind for new ideas and stressing, stretching, scattering the ideas, for better living.

Scientific development is the means of progress. Whatever man has acquired, accomplished, achieved is because of his endeavour to unfold the mysteries of Nature. Advancement in the industrial experience helps to diminish poverty. Progress in medical science eradicates diseases. Achievements in technical knowledge reduce cost and labour.

- When a silkworm disease threatened the French silk industry, **Louis Marie Hilaire Bernigaud de Chardonnet** developed artificial silk (Rayon), then there was acetate Rayon... then Nylon in 1931. Rayon... Nylon... Cloth... Industries.....

  Knowledge to clothe people...

- **Dr. Prafulla Chandra Ray**, an Indian scientist, started making medicinal drugs when he found the medicines from abroad (before independence), too expensive. He attempted and succeeded in setting up a pharmaceutical industry in 1901 and gave indigenous medicines to his countrymen at cheaper, affordable prices.

  Knowledge to treat the people...

- **Alexander Fleming**, when he volunteered for duty in the British army during the First World War, was shocked to see the wounded people. He was deeply troubled, and after the war, he researched in his lab – discovered pencillin in 1928, an antibiotic that revolutionised the medicine world.
  Knowledge to eradicate diseases...

- In 1938, American inventor **Chester Floyd Carlson** affixed a dry, powdered pigment to paper. Then using light and heat, produced a copy...invention of copier...... Xerox......

Knowledge put to use...to reduce cost and labour.

Our material existence is nothing but the interrelation and correlation of different parts of Nature, of universe – investigated, experimented, tried and tested – finally to be used.

> *Where no interest is taken in science,*
> *literature and liberal pursuit,*
> *mere facts and insignificant criticism*
> *necessarily becomes the theme of discourse.*
> *—Madame de Stael*

If time, money and energy is well spent, there is nothing that you can't achieve. Being on the right track, thinking the right thing, doing the right action, for the right purpose – is the power of true knowledge. It is something like – *be a soil scientist or a farmer, but think to yield better.* For every problem there is solution, if you dare to find. Thus, try to know what you don't know, try to learn what you need.

> *To know that we know what we know,*
> *and that we do not know what we do not know,*
> *is true knowledge.*
> —*Henry David Thoreau*

Educate yourself in the way you choose, gain knowledge in the way you like, build your character in the way you decide, develop your intellect in the way you plan, achieve your success in the way you think. Think, read, discuss – the things that matter, for your life and the life of your nation, that is higher, truer, nobler education.

> *Education is a companion no misfortune can decrease,*
> *no crime destroy, no enemy can take away.*
> *At home a friend, abroad an introduction,*
> *in solitude a solace, in society an ornament.*
> *It chastens vice, guides virtue and gives grace to genius.*
> *Education may cost financial sacrifice but in both money*
> *and life values, it will repay every cost hundredfold.*
> *The doorstep to the temple of wisdom is the knowledge*
> *of our own ignorance.*
> —*Charles H. Spurgeon*

You can do it for yourself

1. What does education mean to you, personally?

_____

_____

_____

_____

_____

_____

2. In what way can you educate yourself?

_____

_____

_____

_____

_____

3. In what way can you gain knowledge?

_____

_____

_____

_____

_____

_____

හ ශ

CAN for a Better Nation

Where there is no vision, people perish.....
Where there is vision, people flourish....
—Proverb by King Solomon

*I*ndia is a great country. We are proud to be INDIANS. We are independent, but interdependent. We are independent but interrelated – that is why, it is everyone's contribution which can make INDIA a greater nation. Our country belongs to us all, thus it demands everyone's contribution. *The strength of a nation rests on its individuals and the hope lies with the young minds, like you.* When you achieve, the nation achieves, when you prosper, the nation prospers. You can change the nation – for better, for greater – to make it more powerful, more rich. Your united effort with will and skill can achieve any task ahead.

A mountain can be moved. If not, it can be passed through.

When you are on a journey, have you ever passed through a railway tunnel?

How do you feel?

There are plains **on** land, bridges **on** rivers, tunnels **through** mountains that make miles and miles of railwaytracks, for your transport, for your convenience. A large network! When people visualise mountains, its size, its height, they fear and fail to reach the desired end. When they **do go** – they pass through – to reach their goal.

Going with the tales, believing the opinions, listening to the remarks – we may find, we may discuss, we may evaluate a hundred faults, a hundred errors, but not a single remedy. Our path of freedom is the path of progress, achievement, advancement, accomplishment, attainment – for you and for others, for one and for all, for class and for mass.

If others can improve, others can develop, others can prosper, why can't we?

It needs concern, a thought and an effort.

There may be lack of facilities, scarcity of funds, insufficiency of opportunities, there may be problems, dilemmas, puzzles, there may be obstacles, hurdles, barriers – but aren't we, in some way or the other, directly or indirectly, actively or inactively responsible for that. Every individual is responsible for the community. Individuals make community. *If our community is so....we have made it so.*

You can have a different community, you will have a different nation, more better and more greater – if you act, and not when you fail to act. If you change yourself, your generation changes and you can have better living conditions, better life, better environment, maybe after three years or five years, or even after a decade. Keep the goal to do something to free the men – from poverty, from illiteracy, from diseases. Have the vision to solve the problem of pollution and population – in your generation. **Start from you.** You are a part of the whole. Problems are there because opportunity is not there. Advancement in every sphere is not there because effort, belief, thought is not there in the mind of every individual. Everyone, being responsible – can change the face of himself, so also the face of the nation.

In spite of every problem –

We can be proud of our rich heritage,
rich natural resources, and the most powerful human
resource of one hundred crores and much more...which....

....can be converted to **"Talent and Potential Pool."**

Think up your wellness, so also of others.

Do something for yourself, so also for others.

Be successful, be rich, be prosperous and make others so. Don't think up weakness. Think up strength. Develop the ability. Surmount the difficulty. Try not to fail. Stop not when you fail.

You can't run away from a weakness,
you must sometime fight it out,
and if that be so,
why not now and from where you stand.

A little extra attempt, a little extra effort, a little extra persistence can make it possible. Face your life! Face it!

Not everything that is faced can be changed,
but nothing can be changed until it is faced.
—John Limbo

Realise your power! Develop your potential! Find your purpose!

For the benefit of yourself and the masses at large.

> *Nothing worthwhile is ever achieved without deep thought and hard work. One must strive for excellence in any task, however small, and never be satisfied with the second best. No success or achievement in material terms is worthwhile unless it serves the needs and interests of the country and its people and is achieved by fair and honest means. Good human relations not only bring great rewards but are essential for the success of any enterprise.*
>
> —*J. R. D. Tata*

Get talented to the fullest extent and be an achiever. Look at your career. Watch the people. Examine Nature. Be calm in determination and bold in your effort. Give a promise for the future. Work with focussed attention – to be triumphant, to be victorious. Create a safe, healthy, rich environment. Be active and achieve. Act with imagination, with vision. Work honestly, efficiently, intelligently. Visualise your country – to be better. It is your responsibility to make it so. **You have the freedom of thought, freedom of increasing ability, freedom of action for the benefit of the country.**

> *My faith is in the human intellect; it gives us our means to create wealth by directing our talents towards productive work, and freedom for individual ability is the only way a society can prosper.*
>
> —*L. R. Kirloskar*

Human intellect is so powerful!

Human mind is so powerful!

Human being is so powerful!

Believe that universal power is with you. With that – you can succeed. Without that – you can't. Develop a concern – you can have a solution. Commit today – you can complete tomorrow. In every undertaking there are temporary defeats, temporary setbacks. Don't be worried when you face them, neither limit your thinking in order to retard progress.

Maybe you have to work – a little more time,

Maybe you have to take – a little more help,

Maybe you have to spend – a little more money.

But do it! Do it for yourself! Do it for your nation!

Your talent can build wealth for you! For others!

English scientist **Michael Faraday**, in 1831, proved that vibrations of metal could be converted into electrical impulses. **Johann Philip Reis** in Germany built an apparatus which changed sound to electricity and back. In 1876 **Alexander Graham Bell**, and **Elisha Gray** in USA, independently invented the practical telephone. **Alexander Bell** was ahead, by **two hours** for the patent!

A great competition for achievement!

Then, there were mobile phones for New York Police... then cellular phones in 1981 in USA... then other countries ... other parts... other places... throughout the world.... Think of the communication facility today....

Think of the companies manufacturing cellular phones today.... Think of the Industries.... Factories....

Offices.... Business houses.....
Employees....   Wholesalers.....
Distributors.....   Retailers........
Shops..... Counters.... Facilities....
Utilities.... **Wealth! Employment!**

All for human race, throughout
the world.... A splendid achievement!
For you, for me, for everyone.....

Right at this moment, when you are
reading this page, somewhere, somebody, might be
working hard to make a cellular phone of a different
kind, a little better.....

*Hats off to Michael Faraday, to Graham Bell, to the people
involved.* Their talent created wealth for many people
everywhere. So also ....**Your talent...Can....**

The universe is composed of matter and energy, and
filled with life and power. Power and knowledge – you
can have it everywhere you think. You can use it –
everywhere you plan. It is your responsibility to think of
your life, and it is your duty and privilege to think of the
life of the nation. *You can be somebody, or nobody – by
doing or undoing.* Discipline yourself with morality and
truth – and examine your goal before you begin. Adapt
yourself. Uplift yourself. Upright yourself. Never be
hopeless. Never be thoughtless. Never think of lagging
behind. Improve yourself. Help yourself. **God helps those
who help themselves.** Be sure – your well-meaning,
well-strived effort will never go in vain. Take the guidance
from elderly people. Take the support from your own
men. Take the help from men in office. Ask for help!
Pray to God. Think ahead. *Give your talent and build
a better nation.*

You can think... can grow with the dream...

- For a better life for yourself and a better living condition for different people, in different parts of the nation.
- *Our per capita income is much less than – USA, Japan, Germany and other developed countries.*
- For your personal financial independence and economic advancement for all.
- *Think of economic success – of Japan, Singapore, Germany, USA.*
- For setting up industries and more industrial development.
- *City dwellers should think of rural population and rural mass should think of giving their best for the welfare of the nation.*
- For inventing, discovering and advancing as a nation.
- *Think about the inventions we use in our daily life. Can you not invent? Can you not discover?*
- For taking part in scientific research and technological progress.
- *We have come a long way – but still have a long way to go.*
- For excelling in sports, in games, global participation in Football, Hockey, Badminton, Tennis, Swimming, Cricket.
- *Consider other games, sports, as you chase Cricket......*
- For excelling in Olympics.
- *Remember the performance at the last Olympics.*

- For making a place in the world, performing great in Poetry, Drama, Music, Painting, Cinema, Writing.
— *You have enough talent!*
- For making valuable contribution in afforestation, in green revolution.
— *When the pollution is caused by all – can it be checked by some? Change the proportion of the "Planting Community". Be a planter!*
- For maintaining better standard in health and sanitation.
— *Be aware, make aware, cultivating health is better than treating diseases.*
- For improving agricultural condition, food surplus, yielding better crops by technological advancement.
— *Never forget, whatever you do, however you live – you take lunch and dinner – with the help of a farmer....*
  Remember the farming community and think of advancing them by your talent......
- For living a value-based life and creating an ethical environment.
— *You can be optimistic. Start from you.*
- For peace, progress, prosperity for one and all.
— *Believe in God, believe in yourself.*
- Yes, you can grow with the dream, to be a leader like **Mahatma Gandhi**, a scientist like **C. V. Raman**, a mathematician like **Ramanujam**, a poet like **Rabindra Nath Tagore**, a swimmer like **Mihir Sen**, an astronaut like **Kalpana Chawla** and a cricketer like **Sachin Tendulkar**. The list is endless.....

Continue the list............

You can do it for yourself

1. How do you feel being an INDIAN?

   _____

   2. What do you know about INDIA?

   Population _____

   Men _____

   Women _____

   Literacy rate _____

   People below Poverty line (%) _____

   People living in Cities, in urban area (%)

   _____

   People living in Villages, in rural area (%)

   _____

3. Do you keep your eyes open to know the current
   affairs, issues, events, affecting our lives?

   _____

   _____

4. What do you think about the _____

   Past _____

   Present _____

   Future _____ of India.

5. Who are the Indian personalities you admire from the past, and why?

_____

_____

_____

6. Who are the Indian personalities you admire from the present, and why?

_____

_____

_____

7. Who are your favourite scientists and why?

_____

_____

8. How many software engineers of Indian origin are working abroad?

_____

_____

9. Do you ever wonder how the carpenter, plumber, mason, cobbler, mechanic, slum dweller, rag picker live a life?

_____

_____

10. Can you imagine, can you ever find a permanent solution for the floods and famines the nation faces?

_____

_____

11. Apart from reading, what is your next interest?

_____

_____

12. What can you do for your country?

_____

_____

_____

ಬ ಚ

CAN in Use...

Give to the world the best you have,
and the best will come back to you.

—Anonymous

*Y*our ability to achieve is improved tremendously when you believe that **you can.** Unless you believe, you don't think of undertaking it, let alone trying. You can train to invigorate your belief system for numerous activities, which will lead you to fulfil your goals.

1st Level

CAN is used for the seemingly impossible, and not at all for what you think you can't. You don't dare even to think, taking it as impossible. All the inventions and discoveries were considered impossible at one point of time, during one phase of time. Even if considered possible, they did not happen overnight. First a thought, an idea, then the effort to realise the idea. Accumulated knowledge – experience in the particular field is again and again referred to, researched, experimented, tried, to reach the desired end – with practice, patience, and perseverance. Certain principles, laws, facts – then advancement – *one makes the way for others.*

- **The Montgolfier brothers** made the way for – **the Wright brothers**.

- **Johann Gutenberg**'s printing concept made the way for the typographer, which paved the way for electric – then electronic typewriter.

- **Marco Polo**'s achievement – helped **Columbus** to discover America.

From abacus to laptop... palmtop – is a long way.

Involvement, effort, of many, leads to one, then to another. The inventor or discoverer endeavours wholeheartedly to complete his mission, even when the whole world might be taking and talking of it as impossible. The universal power supports, helps the hard worker through ideas, hunches, intuitions – but the essential ingredient is the belief that he can...who imagines himself to be an inventor and imagines his invention. The spirit of doing something new, something different is backed by belief. You can dare to invent, dare to discover, if you think you can. You can dare to dream the impossible, if you think you CAN.

2nd Level

CAN is used here not for the seemingly impossible, but for a difficult task, which has been already accomplished by someone, by some people, somewhere on Earth, as human beings. Here, CAN is used with respect for the role model or models.

The power of CAN helps to think.

If they could.... Why can't we? – So Can We.

If he could ... Why can't I? – So Can I.

If they can..... Why can't we? – So Can We.

If he can..... Why can't I? – So Can I.

Following the successful people, following the principles of success and striving hard, not as a matter of imitation, rather as a matter of conviction, to live a life like them, to achieve something like them – can be possible with the power of CAN.

3rd level

CAN is used for one and all, who wants to better himself, improve himself, excel himself, even little by little, with devotion and dedication – to increase his efficiency, expand his potentiality, refine his integrity. Anyone can think a little better, can do a little better, can perform a little better.... if he thinks he CAN.

Dr. Emile Coue's principle – **"Every day, in every way, I am getting better and better"** applies to *everyone, in every area of life.*

Be a self starter – follow the power of CAN.

Start... right now....by believing..... "I can do it".... then act and say "I am doing it".... I believe, one day, **you will surely find you have done it!**

ॐ ॐ

CAN
or
Can't

*Y*our success depends on – your efforts.

(How you act, what you do, how you spend your time, how you learn.... how you manage yourself).

You can achieve success....

— When you act to be courageous,
— When you determine to be committed,
— When you wish to be optimistic,
— When you energise to be enthusiastic,
— When you manage to be disciplined,
— When you learn to be competent,
— When you endure to be persistent.....

Your efforts depend on – your feelings.

(The way you feel, the way you respond, the way you view your career, your life).

You can make efforts for success....

— When you feel to be responsible,
— When you feel to be concerned,
— When you feel to be sensitive,
— When you feel to be curious,
— When you feel to be creative.....

Your feelings depend on – your belief.

(The things, the hope, the expectation – what you accept mentally, even though it is not viewed physically, speak about your belief).

You can feel for efforts....

— When you believe...you are someone,
— When you believe... you can,
— When you believe... God is with you....

Your belief depends on – your state of mind.

You can – or – You can't

Your state of mind, condition of mind depends on what you have told to your brain, what you have fed to your brain, how you have programmed your brain – all these years – and that on the other hand depends on what you have listened from others, what you have watched in your surroundings, what you have experienced from your environment. Most of the time you fail to think, fail to accept, fail to believe because your brain is trained, conditioned, programmed **most** for – what you can't do, what you can't expect, what you can't believe in – with all the **how you can'ts** and **why you can'ts** ....

Research says that by the time we are eighteen –

The scenes we see, telling us **No... Can't** – are in thousands... the talks we listen from others, telling us **No.... Can't** – are in lakhs...Basing on that, the talks we talk to our brain (accept silently) are around eighty percent of our total talk, which are negative, anti-productive. Simply put, they work against us.

These we learn – when they come as words, sentences, commands, opinions, remarks, directions – from our brothers, sisters, parents, relatives, teachers, well-wishers – in the name of protection, advice, suggestion, warning, guidance – willingly or unwillingly, planned or unplanned, intentionally or casually.

Our sense organs – specially our eyes and ears – absorb, experience, educate our brain accordingly – at home, in class, in the market, on the playground, inside or outside – in every possible place and from every possible source.

The diary of an ordinary child goes like this....

Early in the morning, his dad wakes him up –

"You lazy ...you're never determined to get up early... and study"....

Mom joins –

"He is always like that. I wish he could have been a bit better"....

The child gets up, brushes his teeth, takes a bath, reads for some time, then prepares for school. On his way to school, he interacts with his mates. One of them consoles....

"You look pale, don't worry, I believe things are not happening right for you. But what more you can do?"

The child attends the classes, one after another. During one class, the teacher warns all – *"If you don't work hard, you can't improve, and you can't do well in exams."*

When school is over, the child returns home. Grabs an afternoon snack and leaves for the playground. There he meets one of his friends, who during a talk, opines –

"We can't afford to be so and so, however hard we may try"....

After some games, some fun, he returns home, washes himself, and sits for the evening study.

Then the tutor arrives, starts teaching, gets worried while checking the home task and shouts at him – *"You seem to be very irresponsible, you just can't do anything right."* After spending an hour and a half, the tutor leaves. A little later, there arrives one of his uncles, his dad's friend. Dad gets busy with uncle. They are engrossed in a conversation relating to opportunity, the essence of which is – *"There is no opportunity, nowhere ...nothing seems possible... now-a-days... unless one has sufficient talent."*

In this way..... a day in the life of a child passed. The child never knew to guard his conscious mind. He has taken all the sentences – without any control. By the end of the day, his *mental computer* has stored....

  i. I'm lazy, I can never be determined.

 ii. I'm always like that – (I'm always lazy), my mother wishes I should have changed my habit.

iii. Things are not happening right for me.

iv. If I don't work hard, I can't improve, and if I can't improve, I can't do well in exams, and because I am lazy – because I am always lazy – and because things are not happening right – I can't work hard and change myself.

v. I can't afford to be so and so even if I try hard.

vi. I am irresponsible, I can't do anything right.

vii. There is no opportunity for me – because I don't have talent – because I am irresponsible, because I am... lazy....

Either the child decides not to be lazy... or in most cases, he accepts himself – to be lazy....

Either we grow being punished, being warned, being restricted or else we grow with laughter, interest, creativity and fun OR a combination of both, OR at one moment with this, and the next with that. The above scene might be the example of a total negative environment, but in standard positive surroundings also, **Nos** and **Can'ts** are dominant, consisting atleast two-thirds of our total talk. Sentences like "No...you can't afford, No... how dare you think so, No... it is not possible here, No...you can't handle it, No... you don't seem to be creative...If only...you were with inborn talent...No... it is not up to your mark.. and so on...and so on ....seem to be only too common. Now just imagine a situation when one after another, five or ten, or more of your friends make fun, by telling you that *you look sick* (even though you are not).... how would you feel? I am sure, you will protest against one, then two, then three, may be eight of them, maybe even ten...... but if it goes more than that, then ....you will gradually start feeling so....... (please don't try it for fun), but you can easily visualise, **how suggestion works**. So when we listen to all can'ts...... all nos..... word by word, we accept all these and tune, direct, suggest our brain. Thinking upon it regularly, frequently, habitually, it passes, sinks into our subconscious mind, where it is collected, piled, preserved – permanently. We begin to think, feel, follow and act accordingly. The more and more we see, the more and more we listen – everything passes into and sticks to respective old thoughts, stored in the same file, the same cabinet of our mental storehouse, to remind us the Nos and the Can'ts...

When we come across a road accident, what do we remember? – All the accidents we had come across earlier. Where do we store the present accident? In the same file, to be recalled by the brain in entirety in the future.

When we come across a new statement, a new idea, a new thought, our brain takes it – scans through the files and cabinets filled with the ideas, impressions, thoughts – and basing upon that, it tells us to accept it or reject it – to believe it or not to believe it, and according to our programming, very often it tells us to say.... No.... Can't.

Can an illiterate resident in a remote village, who is unaware of the fact that man has landed on the Moon, believe that anyone can reach the Moon? Of course not!

Because – he finds it an alien thought, a strange fact, an unfamiliar hope. His mind can't approve it – *as there is nothing in his mind in relation to support it.* On the other hand, it is the belief which can make someone try hard, prepare enough, equip adequately – to be on the Moon, even for seconds.

The most important thing is not why and how we are programmed, but to know, to realise, to conclude that we get back what we put into our brains. **To get back something different – we need to put in something different.** Be happy that your brain can do anything possible, if you tell it to do strongly, regularly, sincerely, (not necessarily lakhs of times) to create a better you, *irrespective of what you have been in the past or what you are today.*

You can counter the negative suggestions,

You can guard your conscious mind,

You can replace the negative with strong positive words,

You can recondition, retrain, reprogram your mind to control you, guide you, direct you – to believe, to achieve.

Believe it and go through the book – to believe in yourself ..... For a better and greater life....

When you listen from others/from inside	You convert it	You command – your brain to accept...
1. You are lazy	I can be active	I am active
2. You are irresponsible	I can be responsible	I am responsible
3. You do not have talent	I can be talented	I am growing in talent
4. You are poor in every respect	I can be rich in every respect	I am getting richer in every respect
5. Things are not happening right for you	I can be unaffected by the things. I can control myself	I am controlling myself
6. You can't find any opportunity	I can find, make, create many opportunities	I find many opportunities
7. You can't succeed	I can succeed	I am on the way to success

You can do it for yourself

Believe it – Practice it – By Repeated Suggestion – (Silent or aloud) and see how you feel in your daily life.

Don't worry for the action, in the first place.

I think and believe I can achieve success in my life.

I realise the power of decision and action.

I decide and take full responsibility of my life.

I educate myself and gain knowledge every day, in every way.

I think and act for a better nation.

I dream and work hard to realise my dream.

I am on the way to achieve success, in my career.

I am working hard to live a meaningful life.

(Read it, as often as you can)
Change your words... Change your life...

ऄ अ

Section-II

YOU
CAN BUILD
A BETTER YOU

"You should build a better world," God said,
He questioned, "How?"
"The world is such a wondrous place,
So complicated now!
And so small and useless am,
There is nothing I can do,"
But God, all-wise and kind replied,
"Just build a better you."

—*Anonymous*

Believe in GOD

When we really love God,
then existence is not something,
it is some one,
it is not just living, it is loving.

Who are YOU?

You are one in the universe, one with the universe, one amidst the universe. You have it and it has you. You are with it and it is with you. You are of it and it is for you. The same power which created the universe created YOU – and it is the power of your Creator, your Maker, your Master Designer.......**God**.

All these days you might be busy with your daily errands, all these days you might be worried with "What I can", "What if I can', or "If only I could". All these days you might never have chanced to look at the sky, to think about the endless universe... .. But, you know about the limitless universe, the galaxies, the comets, the asteroids, the planets, the stars, being miles and miles away – the distance of which can only be measured in light years. The light from some of them even takes years to reach the Earth.

The rotation of Earth, the revolution of Earth and other planets, the movement of other heavenly bodies, the appearance of Halley's Comet,... can be foretold.

The Sun is placed at an exact distance – neither a little closer to burn you up, nor a little farther to freeze you. The planets are directed to revolve, in their respective orbits, to avoid crashing into each other. The oceans, the continents, the landmass and the water bodies are well demarcated. The atmosphere or the environment is made up of elements, mixed in a certain proportion to suit you.

The Sun rises in the east and sets in the west.....

Carnivores depend on herbivores......

Birds migrate before spring......

A frog grows out of a fish-like tadpole......

Sheep move away before the severe storm......

Field mice seal up their holes before the cold weather......

Tortoises retire to rest and take refuge before every shower of rain......

Vultures cover miles of distance to reach the dead animal......

A butterfly moves constantly......

An ant never stops and is never alone......

A small mango seed grows into a huge mango tree......

A baby elephant grows into a big one......

A baby child, like you, grew – to be a **young you**...... Upward.... Lifeward....Godward.... following the law of Nature.

Every creation, every being, from the tiny micro-organism to the huge elephant, every body, heavenly or earthly – in the oceans, or in the seas – are well-placed, well-ordered, well-directed, expressing the amazing power of our Creator – and creation – wonderful, astonishing and mysterious.

Did it just happen ..... in course of time?

Did it just happen ..... as a matter of chance?

Did it just happen ..... as a matter of coincidence?

Can you find anything..... that just happened?

Your home, your car, your bicycle, or your television, anything....nothing in this universe just happens. Nothing is just well-ordered, just well-placed, just well-directed.

God's absence is an illusion. All the things in Nature speak of the greatness of – the Creator, the Maker, the Master Designer.

Science does help us to know what God has made and what God can make. Science does not create anything out of nothing. It does so out of God's creation. It does with God's power, the universal power that creates, that dissolves and that recreates.

Every new discovery of Science is a further revelation of the order that God has built into his Universe.
                              —Warren Weaver

God – the Omnipotent, the Omniscient, the Omnipresent. God is Truth, God is Love. God is Light, God is Life. He gives life and draws the bottom line – of you, of me, of everyone. His power – universal power.

His intelligence – infinite intelligence. His wisdom – indispensable wisdom.

He is the source of all power, all energy, 'all' means all – solar energy, sound energy, heat energy, nuclear energy. We know that energy can neither be created (by us!), nor can it be destroyed (by us!). It can only be transformed (by us!) from one form to another. Energy remains energy – forever and the source of energy is – everlasting God.

His power is thus scattered through like the talks of the cellular phone, and in that power, with that power, in the midst of that power, I live, you live, a life – with your body and soul.

Your body is temporal, your soul is immortal – it remains inside you. It always thinks to link with God and more so when you are distressed, disillusioned, disappointed. All that time, you get closer to God crying: "Oh my God!" Your body might be in need of something usual or unusual, good or bad, worthy or unworthy, but your soul is satisfied with spiritual food. Your soul, when in communion with God – has a higher, inner power which leads you, guides you, controls you to lead a **just** life, a **righteous** life, a **holy** life.

When you fail to nourish your soul, it is embittered, unsettled and makes you restless. Everything seems impossible to you. But with Him, everything is possible. Believe in Him. Believe in His power.

Knowing about Him is not sufficient, rather, know Him personally. He is the Supreme Authority, the Greatest Ruler, the Master Protector of your life.

When your thoughts are good, filled with love, kindness, goodwill, joy, happiness, hope, and faith, He is with you.

He fills you with enough power, enough wisdom, enough knowledge and enough patience. *Knowledge and humility are the wealth of soul* – let them go hand in hand. Have faith in God – to find the path of a better life. Have faith in God – to achieve, to accomplish, to invent, to discover. Have faith in God – to overcome frustration, anxiety, worry, tension, depression.

Faith is not a matter of intelligence, neither a matter of intellect, nor reason. It is to build within, it has to spring from, it has to come from the core of your inner part – your heart.

Bitterness, worry, resentment, hostility, guilt, selfishness, suspicion, pride, injustice – are the result of lack of faith in God.

When you are troubled, dismayed, distressed, criticised, fatigued, defeated, crushed, failed.....

Have faith in God.....

There .... **Faith** acts as a flash of light in darkness.

The source of faith is God,
The companion of faith is hope,
The channel of faith is prayer,
The partner of faith is action,
The evidence of faith is obedience,
The beauty of faith is miracle,
The result of faith is change,
The reward of faith is growth,
The expression of faith is service,
The path of faith is joy.
—*William Arthur Ward*

Faith is the vital force to prompt a significant change. Faith is the abundance of power. Faith is the master key for your success. Faith is the determinant of your progress. Faith overcomes all barriers, all limitations. Faith is the panacea of the mind.

Faith is strength to counter – worry, fear and anxiety. Faith is hope. Faith is life. Faith is the consciousness of a living God.

It is the faith that steers us through stormy seas, faith that moves mountains and faith that jumps across the ocean. That faith is nothing but a living wide-awake consciousness of God within. He who has achieved that faith wants nothing.
—*Mahatma Gandhi*

When you have faith in Him, you are under His Grace.

If anything is above you, it is still under His feet.

His power is for you. His intelligence is with you. He is above you, with you, for you. Contact Him, communicate with Him, tell Him, pray to Him.

More things are wrought by prayer than this world can dream of.
—*Alfred Tennyson*

Prayer is communication with God – expressing thankfulness or asking blessings. It is a welcome to God to enter in you. It is a supplication to fulfil your aim, your ambition, your goal. It is an effort to seek advice. It is an attempt to get comfort in times of trouble. It is a commitment to follow Him. It is a method to purify the outer and the inner. It is a way to be controlled, to be guided, to be led. It is a pledge to live under His grace. It is a quest – to know the purpose of life and to achieve a higher end with His power.

> *Prayer is the most powerful form of energy one can generate, it is a force as real as terrestrial gravity. Prayer, like radium, is a source of luminous, self-generating energy..... In prayer, human beings seek to augment their finite energy by addressing themselves to the infinite source of all energy. When we pray, we link ourselves with the inexhaustible motive power that spins the universe. We pray that a part of this power be apportioned, to our needs. Even in asking, our human deficiencies are filled, and we arise strengthened and repaired ...*
> *When we address God in fervent prayer, we change both soul and body for the better.*
> —*Dr. Alexis Carrel*

Prayer is not mere lip service. It is not a matter of uttering articulated, good words. It is not a well-evaluated, bargaining or calculation. It is **'what springs out with utmost faith in the power of God'.**

Most of the people fail, even as they pray – because they doubt God.

If they doubt Him, if they expect failure, even with Him, if they accept **can't** even while praying to Him, *who else is left to answer them?*

Have faith in God. Accept in your mind – He is with you, He is guiding you, He is protecting you, He is enfolding you, He is watching you. Live a life to the fullest – to keep your record true, to be evaluated by your Master Scorer.

His guidance – will guide you, to live happily,

His comfort – will provide you peace, solace,

His light – will lead you......

Lead kindly Light, amid the encircling gloom,
lead thou me on;
The night is dark, and I am far from home;
lead thou me on.
Keep thou my feet;
I do not ask to see the distant scene;
one step enough for me.

—Cardinal Newman

One step...

Then the next....and another...till you achieve.

Your faith can help you to dream....even to do the impossible.....to feel the intangible.....

You can think beyond your grasp and still can feel confident to succeed. You can develop all sincerity to satisfy God, who will fulfil your dream and your desire. You can build enough wisdom and enough patience to be afirmative in your day to day life and can be sure that with Divine power, no way are you doomed for disappointment....

Do great for the whole of mankind, and your life will be a life of joy and happiness.

Some of the time you may find it tough to proceed, difficult to endure, harassed to continue...but remember, always, that the Divine power is with you – to surmount all the difficulties. Never fear to do anything worthwhile, never feel discouraged, never feel inferior.

If you have guilt – God will forgive you. If you are weak – God will strengthen you. If you are ashamed – God will glorify you.

He alone is Almighty – not the difficulties you face, the problems you go through, or the people who laugh at you.

Along with his strength only you can cope with the inevitable, live without the indispensable, bear with the intolerable. So be happy.....and be sure.

He can remake you. He can rebuild you. He can recreate you.

You can feel Him. You can hear Him. You can experience Him.

You don't see the electricity, but see the light,

You don't see the wind, but feel it,

You don't see God, but you believe in Him.....

Ask Him, depend on Him, pray to Him.

You can do something, you can achieve something, you can accomplish something ..... in life.

> *To accomplish great things,*
> *we must not only act but also dream,*
> *not only plan but also believe.*

> *—Anatole France*

৯০ ଓଃ

Know your Purpose

What a piece of work is man!
How noble in reason! How infinite in faculties!
In form and moving how express and admirable!
In action, how like an angel!
In apprehension how like a god!
—William Shakespeare

Non-living and living, plants and animals, are all created, designed, shaped by God. The complex life process of every creation, not only you, but even the unicellular micro-organism is also astonishing. Cells → tissues → organs → body. Every one has millions and millions of cells with specific task, special function, unique responsibility to carry on various life processes.

Not every species, but every individual like you is – special, unique, different – before God.

Two leaves are different...

Two zebras are different...

Two human beings are different...

Your face and features are different from others...

Your finger print is different from others...

Your DNA is different from others...

Millions and millions of human beings are there on this Earth – but *nobody is like you.* Considering the number of chromosomes which comprise numerous genes, genetics informs us that even in your family, there could have been many more brothers and sisters, in millions, and even that be so, all would have been totally different from each other. Every creation is different.

God created every individual different, unique, special. So also you! With great care... for what? A purpose – good or bad, respectful or not, worthy or unworthy? I believe – definitely for something good, something beautiful, something virtuous – for a worthy goal. To live a human life, for others, for other human beings, for the glory of God.

Every person must have a concern for self and feel a responsibility to discover his mission in life. God has given each normal person a capacity to achieve some end. True, some are endowed with more talent than others, but God has left none of us talentless. Potential powers of creativity are within us and we have the duty to work assiduously to discover the power.

—Martin Luther King

Everyone can teach you how to walk but it is not sufficient. It mostly depends on you – which path you take, what purpose you live for, what steps you should, you can, you will take, to realise your purpose, your mission, your goal, either in harmony with God to live in joy and happiness *or* drifting away from God – to meet disappointment, disease, depression, hampering spiritual, mental and physical health – through the passage of life.

It depends how you travel in the journey of life, it depends how you act in the drama of life, it depends how you play the game of life.

> *For when the One Great Scorer,*
> *comes to write against your name,*
> *He marks not that you won or lost –*
> *but how you played the game.*
>
> —*Grantland Rice*

Believe in Him. You are different. You are important. **Start being you.** Let your life be a quest for understanding the real purpose of your existence. Live a life with eagerness, with joy, with zest. *God has given rules for healthy living. God has given principles for the purity of soul. God has given laws for caring the universe, caring the life.* Adhere to them. Be with God. Believe in Him. Have faith in Him. Your opinion, your discernment, your judgement, your decision may help you to move with God or away from God. Value His assignment, His expectation, His prescription. *Get into the beautiful world and live for a worthy goal.* That is your purpose.

How can you fulfil a purpose? How does a sculptor get an elephant out of a huge rock? He cuts the unnecessary parts, keeps the necessary and does the finishing, shapes the trunk, head, nose, eyes and gets

– a superb, marvellous stone-cut elephant. So can you! Keep the good, avoid the bad, keep the need, avoid the greed, keep the virtue, avoid the vice, hone what you keep. Over... Purpose fulfilled...that is it!

I am one, but still I am one,
I can't do everything, but I can do something,
and what I should and can do,
by the Grace of God, I will do.

—Edward Everette Helle

You can do it for yourself

I believe in God and in His power. I understand that He has a brilliant idea, and a grand purpose for me, for my life. I believe I can and I am on the way to find and fulfil the purpose, with the help of His power. I don't find anything impossible, because for God everything is possible. I read, I study, I learn, I grow, I work, I play. I make wholehearted attempts with all my effort. I forgive and forget. I am never worried nor afraid. I am not selfish, not suspicious, not escapist, not egotist, not impatient, not arrogant. I never backbite, never criticise. I hate hypocrisy, shun jealousy.

But....

I am cordial, gentle and humble, I am loving, caring and winning. I thank God, worship God, pray to God, praise God, for his sufficient blessings and abundant grace – for my creation.

I live a life for myself, my family, my community and my nation and for the whole of mankind.

I consult God as I consult Dad, today, tomorrow and forever, from this timeforth till I breathe my last.

(Read this everyday, remember this every moment.)

୫ଓ ଓ୫

Care your Body

Glorify God in your body and in your spirit,
which are God's.

—Holy Scriptures

*Y*our body is made up of many organs, muscles, bones, tissues, cells. Sense organs help you to smell, taste, feel, look, listen. Organs are there for respiration, digestion, circulation, each for a specific function. You eat, you walk, you respire, you perspire, you read, you listen – with the help of these intricate and complexly designed organs and systems, making you grow to be a healthy human being. You, your soul, your body is a gift of God. It needs care, it needs love. Love your body. Care for your body. Keep it fit. When you are physically fit, everything works better, your performance is better. Specially when you are growing, you must co-operate to grow properly. Cultivating health is much more important than treating diseases. To cultivate health means to look after the need of various organs, various systems and satisfy the need and maintain these, to function properly, using them more and making them better.

Incorrect food habits, lack of exercise, negligence and mis-use hampers health. To be healthy, you need to support your body.

Food Habits:

You must go for a well-balanced diet with protein, fat, carbohydrate, minerals, vitamins and water – in the right proportion. Avoid acidic food, stress upon more alkaline food. See that the food combination is proper. When there is a good combination, digestion takes place easily, properly, giving you energy. Improper food combination causes indigestion, as it takes a long time to digest and till that time you suffer, feel awkward in the stomach. Hyperacidity, acid reflux, flatulence are felt, and on regular, frequent occurrences they lead to gastrointestinal disorders, even ulcers.

Better food combinations are:

i.   *Proteins + Non-starchy Vegetables.*

ii. *Non-starchy Vegetables + Starchy Carbohydrate.*

iii. *Non-starchy Vegetables + Fatty and Oily food.*

- Don't eat proteins with fatty, oily food as it becomes difficult to digest.
- Don't eat fruits with any other food, because fruit goes through your body quickly as it is easily digested, and any other food may block the movement of fruit.
- Don't neglect your breakfast nor take too little and irregularly. It is important – as you are breaking the night's fast.
- Don't eat snacks between meals as they impair digestion and lead to lack of appetite.

- Don't develop a habit of taking fried food and fast food regularly. *Too much of it and too often –* may cause digestive disorders.

- Don't take animal flesh too frequently, as it takes time to be digested.

- Don't eat hurriedly, as less chewing hampers proper digestion.

Drink:

Water is another necessary ingredient, like air, to live a life. About seventy percent of your body is water. On an average you should take eight glasses of water, everyday. Develop a habit of sitting down to drink water.

Water helps in –

i. Digestion	–	Activates the enzymes in the digestive system, prevents constipation.
ii. Respiration	–	Moistens air through nose, till lungs.
iii. Circulation	–	Blood collects water from surrounding.
iv. Lubrication	–	Saliva helps in lubrication of food. Fluid lubricates the eyes. Fluid also cushions the joints.
v. Regulation of Temperature	–	Sweat glands moisten your skin. Evaporation through them helps to cool the body.
vi. Filtration	–	Kidneys and skin excrete poisons. Sufficient water enables the kidneys to function better – to excrete uric acid, urea.

vii. Transportation   –   Helps to carry nutrients and oxygen to the cells through the blood.

- Water taken during mealtime dilutes the gastric juice and also reduces the chewing. Thus, avoid taking water during mealtime. It is best to take it half an hour *before or after* the mealtime.

Other Drinks:

Tea, coffee, cola contains caffeine. In small and moderate dose, it stimulates and improves mental performance. But, is habit-forming and has got ill-effects as it is used as *borrowed energy*. Too much of caffeine increases blood pressure, causes irregular heartbeat, elevates blood sugar– leading to irritation, nervousness, anxiety, depression, and insomnia (sleeplessness). It is not advisable to make it a habit.

- Drink water when you feel like drinking any such beverage.

Exercise:

Regular exercise is good for your health. There are various types of exercises – running, jogging, walking, swimming, skating; games – cricket, football, badminton, hockey, tennis, golf, basketball. Any form of exercise increases the efficiency of different organs, enhances the stamina, develops a defence mechanism and prolongs your life. Choose a form of exercise that suits and interests you.

Exercise –

i. Builds muscles, increases blood supply, enhances the power and efficiency of various organs.

ii. Improves the circulation of blood, strengthens the heart and the lungs (cardio vascular system).

iii. Reduces stress (hypertension) and chances of stress-related diseases.

iv. Strengthens and tones the muscles, joints, ligaments, tendons and firms the calves, buttocks, hips, abdomen, thighs.

v. Helps to control or lose weight.

vi. Helps in digestion, in perspiration.

vii. Helps to sleep better, increases mental efficiency and makes you feel good.

- Exercise should not be too strenuous – to make you *overfatigued nor imbalanced* – to harm your other activities, especially studies.

Breathing:

Correct breathing is essential to be healthy. By breathing, you oxygenate the body, stimulate the cells, eliminate the toxins.

- Breathe through the nose.
- Control your breathing – you can control your emotions.
- To clean the system – practise deep breathing, involving abdomen. Inhale one count to take the

oxygen, hold four counts to oxygenate fully, exhale two counts to eliminate toxins.

Sleep:

Your body needs rest. Rest is repair. Sleeping is a matter of taking rest, and a matter of habit. You must control and keep it – as a healthy habit. Too much sleep is unwise, and too less is harmful. After a good night's sleep, you should awake in the morning fully alert to meet the invitation of the day.

- Sleep seven to eight hours a day. You can manage with six. Less than that is harmful for body and mind.

- Make sleep a good habit – right time to retire to bed, right time to get up. Try to sleep on your side, not on your back.

- Think something good, something productive, something beautiful, something great just before you sleep -- your subconscious will accept it.

Care for your organs:

Eyes:

Your eyes are like a camera. The image that you observe is sensed by your brain and makes you know. Take care of your eyes.

- Don't stare for a long time, blink regularly while studying.

- Sleep properly to give rest to the eyes.

- Be cautious while working with your desktop, laptop, video games – on screen, on mobile and don't watch your television for too long.

Television is a blessing, Internet is a blessing – if used well.

Watch TV for news, for political issues, for economic information, for scientific programmes, regularly, and for entertainment, casually. Scrutinise your TV habits to reject the negative impact, atleast till you grow to be a successful adult. Ask yourself – What is good in it? And never justify and say, *What is wrong in it?* – while you feel to watch anything. If you find something good – go ahead, if not, stay away. Your career, your life is much more important and thus you should distance yourself from everything which may hinder your normal personal growth. Your time, your age, your period of growth – physical and mental – can never be recycled, all other things can be. *Listen to good music to relieve stress and control emotions to make you cheerful.*

Teeth:

Oral hygiene and dental care is important for your body.

- Brush your teeth twice daily.
- Chew properly anything you eat.
- Take milk regularly.

Too much of chocolate, mints, sweets, even oily food – invites bacteria, which harms your teeth. Avoid every form of tobacco. It is bad not only for your teeth, but also for your body. Eat vegetables and fruits for better teeth, better health.

Nose:

Keep it clean. Avoid obstruction and infection. The best way to clean the nose is to shut one nostril, open the mouth and sneeze. Let the inner lining of your nose be clean and healthy.

Ears:

Clean them regularly after a bath and occasionally use ear buds. Never use any other thing. Do protect your ears.

General:

Cut your nails regularly, wash your feet regularly.

Clean your body regularly.

Don't use too much or too intense – perfume, deo, talc.

Take care from tip to toe.

Consult doctors at regular intervals, even when you are not sick.

Avoid Smoking, Avoid Alcohol:

They are the greatest enemy for your body, specially when you are growing. Smoking stunts growth. It affects all the systems of your body. Alcohol is harmful. Unless you are alert and watchful, you will pick it up from 'sometimes' to habit-forming. Say 'No' to start what you may not be able to stop. These things are like a *comfortable bed – easy to get into but hard to get out*.

Give up the habit – if you have it all. Don't love anything at the cost of your health. Be conscious of health, conscious of money, conscious of success, conscious of life. Think! The money you spent could have been used otherwise, *at least to purchase a good book for reading*...for knowledge...for success...for life.

The care you take today can make you a better person tomorrow, with a better personality, liked by all.

Don't nourish the cause today...to get the effect tomorrow.

Take proper care. Maintain good health.

Be fit. Be disease free.

Be free from fear of illness:

Program your mind for better health. When you are mentally sick, you will have all the symptoms – even at the slightest provocation. Most of the diseases are *"psychosomatic"* in nature, built in "psyche"– your mind, to be manifested in "soma" – your body, and a lot more people suffer from imaginary illness – "hypochondria". Get rid of negative emotions – stress, anxiety, fear, and fill your mind with positive thoughts – hope, faith and love. Pray to God, even for the little suffering, the little headache. Believe in Him – to be healed. See yourself in good health. If and when you feel sick, never panic, to aggravate the problem nor go around telling others how bad you feel. Don't fear diseases. Believe that God is with you. Talk to yourself – that you are natural, you are healthy, you are normal. Practise to move your body and balance your body at will. Make use of your body for simultaneous actions. Move your legs, arms and increase your flexibility. Develop a habit to concentrate on your work at hand, making your body strong. Cultivate better health, take care of your body.

> *It is health which is real wealth*
> *and not pieces of gold and silver.*
>
> —*Mahatma Gandhi*

You can do it for yourself

	Food	Drink	Exercise	Breathing	Sleep	Health Harm
		water+other drinks		normal+deep breathing		
SUNDAY						
MONDAY						
TUESDAY						
WEDNESDAY						
THURSDAY						
FRIDAY						
SATURDAY						

Make a note if you deviate and how you deviate.

Keep a record for a week and find how you *differ* from detailed, how you maintain your health.

₧ ₨

Honour your Parents, Educators, Counsellors

I am indebted to my father for living,
but to my teacher for living well.
—Alexander the Great

*Y*our parents, teachers, counsellors are your well-wishers, believe in them. They are the people who are right for you. They are too good when you honour them.

Your career, your success, your life is your duty, their responsibility. Don't blame them, blame is always a losing game, where nobody wins. It is like the game of ringball – thrown from one to the next, then to the other and so on.

Focus on solution. Blame is past, not future. Taking steps for solution is future. I have always experienced, believed – parents are good for you. They hope, believe and expect good. They give their best as they trust you. Thank your parents. Obey your teachers. Listen to your counsellors. Live up to their expectation, their desire, their dream by becoming better. When you are not, you hurt them. How painful it is when you fail to do so, being distracted, deviated!

Sometimes you have to take a tough stand, to stay away from fun, from pleasures. Keep it in mind, your parents love you. When in need, ask for help, they can and they will.

It is the sign of humility. Everyone takes help.

The rewarded scientist takes help of his associates.

The able doctor takes help of nurses, pharmacist.

The qualified teacher takes help of his colleagues.

An efficient officer takes help of his staff.

Everyone lives by helping – or taking help.

There is nothing wrong – if you ask for help.

Your ego, your stubbornness, your fear may stop you from asking, don't listen to it. Sooner or later it will be known to you that you need help. Better to let them know earlier than when it is too late. Tell them clearly, allowing to know – your strength, your weakness.

Let them know –

Your plan, your goal, your desire, your dream.

Be frank even if you are at fault. *To err is human.* Rectify it but never repeat it. Be at ease. Find your deficiency – think and ask for remedy. Admit your need. *Realise where you stand and where you have to go, how you can go, with whose help you can go.*

Human relationships, understanding, dependence are like the cycles of Nature.

Water Cycle: Water from the oceans, seas, lakes → evaporation → cloud → rain → water in the seas, lakes, rivers, oceans.

Oxygen Cycle: We inhale oxygen → exhale carbon dioxide → taken by plants → plants give out oxygen.

Seed → Plant → then fruit → then seed again.

So also your behaviour, your thought, your action, your feelings. *You get back what you give.*

Nothing goes from you, never to return. Throw a ball, it will come back. Throw a word, it will come back.

Love begets love. Hate begets hate.

You do your part – they will do theirs.

Cultivate kindness. That's an art.

Kind words produce kind *echoes* !

Never misinform them nor misquote them.

If you want to be loved – love them.

If you want to be supported – support them.

If you want to be cared for – care for them.

Believe in them. Respect them. Honour them.

Your parents will take care of you – in a better way.

Your teachers will teach you – in a better way.

Your counsellors, well-wishers will guide you – in a better way.

Be together for progress, for success.

Every individual in this world is responsible for his action and behaviour. So are they, and so are you.

Whose life does it really matter?

To make them happy–

   i. Express good manners, exhibit good behaviour.

  ii. Be a good reader, be a greedy reader.

 iii. Be polite – learn vocabulary, use correct words.

 iv. Concentrate to maintain, develop and grow, to succeed.

  v. Be curious – question them.

 vi. Be sensitive – know them, learn from them.

 vii. Be intelligent – to study, to learn, to be useful.

viii. Show cheerfulness and fill yourself with goodness, tolerance and patience.

 ix Avoid a fight. Be accountable for domestic bliss.

  x. Be humorous – to make everyone happy, pleased, contented, and feel happy for you.

Honour them.

You can do it for yourself

Name ten people who really matter to your life. You care for them and they care for you, including your parents, teachers, counsellors, well-wishers, relatives and friends, and **wish them, now!**

1. _____

2. _____

3. _____

4. _____

5. _____

6. _____

7. _____

8. _____

9. _____

10. _____

༄ ༅

Parents, Teachers, Counsellors, Please!!!

The Earth flourishes or is overrun with noxious weeds, and brambles as we apply or withhold the cultivating hand. So fares it with the intellectual system of man. If you are a <u>parent</u>, then consider that the good or ill dispositions and principles you please to cultivate in the mind of your <u>infant</u> may hereafter preserve a nation in prosperity, or hang its fate on the point of the sword.

—Horace Mann

*W*hy only Parents.... Teachers as well.

Why only Infants... Children... Young minds as well.

In the formative years, the words, opinions, remarks, suggestions of parents and teachers influence the mind of growing children. They tend to learn everything from all available sources – at different points of time. These as a whole, shape the life of children and they grow to be young men and women forming the future of a nation. They try to accept, think, believe what they learn from others. They understand what they should and what they shouldn't, what to accept, and what to reject, what is affordable and what is not, what is healthy, what is unhealthy, **what they can, and what they can't.** Gradually, these thoughts settle in their subconscious mind and reflect to express their mental ability or inability – in turn, activity or inactivity. Societal suggestion controls their upbringing and brings out, accordingly, as it is put in. *Parents are the first teachers and teachers are the second parents.* They are the models for the young minds. Young minds not only see what they do, but also how they do. These environmental aspects are impressed upon more than the teachings of the textbooks. Mere study in schools, colleges or institutions can't cultivate the young minds to live a worthy life and on the other side, the day to day affairs and current news headlines do not allow the parents to visualise the distant future. It is a fact that no one can be blind to the present basic need, but isn't it true that it can do no good if one fails to think of the future. Everyone must look to the present, but should think of the future, which comprises the future of their own children. The course of action is the individual and united effort, to have a better environment, better education, better facility, for a better social, cultural and economic order.

Thus, it becomes obligatory for everyone in the society to make a part of the future nation by being active, alert and agile. Every parent, every teacher, every guardian, every custodian of a young mind can decide what he needs in the future or what he wants the country to be like. *Things do not happen, unless and until someone makes them happen. Things do not change, unless and until someone changes. Things do not improve, unless and until someone improves.* It is the duty of the young minds, but the responsibility of parents and teachers.

Everyone should make his child eager to understand the skill to be a **lifter** and not a **leaner**. An atmosphere filled with discouragement, criticism, punishment, often results in the children being more prone to failure and unworthy activities, something *no parent wants, no parent deserves.* By being a little responsible, a little concerned, a little careful, one can not only build a *better child* but can also build a *better nation.*

When the former part of life is misused or ill-spent, it is not only the loss of the child or of the family but the loss of the nation as well. Proper environment, value-based education and correct guidance can help them to **think big and aim high.**

"Practise what you preach" should not be interpreted as – *We can't practise, so, we should not preach.* Many parents stop telling, asking, helping, convincing, managing the children when they grow up, as they can't practise what they preach. Everyone must preach and try hard to practise. When parents fail even to preach, they send the message: "This is not bad", or "Not so bad". Parents expect the children to experience and learn when they grow enough. Can you wait while a child burns his finger and experiences fire? *It is always better if a son realises his father is right before he becomes the father of a son.* A wise son makes a glad father. Parents who are careful enough set examples for their own children by their action, behaviour and words and by doing that, not only do they help the children, but also serve the nation, by creating better citizens. **Not everything is easy, but everything can be possible.** Everyone should try hard to stop the degeneration of the moral fabric of the young generation. Parents who try to support the children by pleasing the teachers for unethical means get undesirable results along with unhappiness, in due course of time. Some of the parents are so sticky to the false belief that – *my child is the best, my child never does that, my child can never be expected to do that.* They, in fact, never come to know what the child really does. It is good to feel proud of the child but at the same time, it is required to keep an inventory of his development – physical, mental and moral. Lack of feeling to control or an absolute faith sometimes encourages the grooming of misdeeds, when the child fails to be loyal. At the same time, excessive pressure aggravates the situation. One has to create a *balance* between the two – and *that is disciplining.*

Disciplining should not be a punishment, rather it should be taken as a tool to improve the child, and not to satisfy the parent's super temper or self-ego. It should be made very clear to the errant child that if he does not improve after disciplining, it will be **his** loss.

Be sure and make sure that –

i.   You are not the cause of his offence.

ii.   You are not doing it to satisfy your temper, your ego.

iii. You are trying for a permanent solution.

I believe they can be well-capable, understandable, educable to do something, do everything for a brighter future.

At home, teach them to accept each other, consider everyone's need and help everyone to solve individual and domestic problems. Maintaining harmony between individuals in a family and catering to their need can train them to be useful in the later stage of life. Quick admission and immediate apology serves to maintain peace and balance. Everyone should be cordial to each other. Home is the place where joy and happiness is taught, practiced, experienced. When children grow to be caring confident, enthusiastic, – they create a good home and build a good life.

Teach them to take responsibility, realising the condition and situation of the home. *A father is the head of the house, and the mother is the heart.* Everyone should develop a habit of talking *to* and never talking *at*. An attitude of 'Talking *at*' creates havoc in the family, in the society, in the community, everywhere. 'Talking *to*' finds solution to every problem and makes a cordial brother and sister, husband and wife, cultivating a strong sense of humour, without expecting perfection, but always encouraging excellence.

Cheating and deceiving mostly start or grow either in the family or in the environment, when a little of it is taken casually, at an early stage, and allowed to continue in a moderate form. The electronic media should be used more for knowledge, less for fun. Teach the children positive ways of life and groom them to be healthy citizens, to be great assets.

Build up the young minds. Fill them with power. Instil dreams, help them fulfil them. Let them experience, let them achieve. Create an inspiring atmosphere of creative activity. Train them. Motivate them. Encourage them. Praise them. Thank them. Get close. Get involved. Spend time with them. Make them self-reliant, caring and loving. Recognise their strength, their weakness and help them improve. Study their behaviour. Watch their company. See them, correct them. *A stitch in time saves nine.* Handle them with care and tend them with hope. Make them self conscious – to be meaningful for them, for you and for the entire nation. Every child is gifted and can bloom to the fullest when you believe in him, and when you help him believe in himself and in the power of the Creator.

Disciplining children involves spending time with them, knowing what they are doing, what they are learning, how they are learning. Or the best thing is to set standards by your own self-image and action. *That really works, and works well.*

He that gives good advice, builds with one hand.
He that gives good counsel and example, builds with both.
But he that gives good admonition and bad example,
builds with one hand and pulls down with the other.
—Francis Bacon

Love them, care for them, discipline them, build them in the midst of fun and laughter, encouragement and accomplishment. Discipline means not to be a judge or a cynic or a pessimist, but *ignorance is not bliss here.* Teaching them to walk is not enough, show them the right path as well. An open atmosphere of trial and error, experience and learn, love and permit, sometimes leads the young mind to commit mistakes, to regret later. Preach the virtues of truth, integrity and work hard. Carelessness brings extreme forms of troubles. Blaming on this and that can never bring a solution. After all, it is your child, your family, your nation. Excessive freedom like excessive pressure, destroys the life of a child. A little pressure is always needed to keep on working. Not all the pressures are bad nor all the punishments worst.

Under pressure over many years, dolomite, a mineral, crystallises into marble. Pressure should not be accompanied with super expectation. **If they are expected to do something, let them be encouraged and enlightened – by all.** To make them resourceful, they must be taught to overcome anxiety, worry, fear, owing to impatience and restlessness. Let not the young minds be so kiddish so as not to understand, not to realise, not to perform anything for self and society in the name of pressure. Rather help them, guide them, counsel them to think, believe and achieve something worthwhile for the people, for the nation.

What is actually required is the making of a new man – someone who has confidence in the limitless possibility of his own development, someone who is not intimidated by the prospect of an open hour; someone who is aware that science may be able to make an easier world but only man can make a better one.

—Norman Cousins

Parents Please!

It is their duty – but your responsibility

1. Build confidence with proper care and understanding.
2. Spend time with them, being attentive.
3. Discipline your own life to set an example to show the right way.
4. Live a happy, positive life and allow them to follow.
5. Promise them and keep it, to inspire, motivate them.
6. Train them for correct manners, habits, language.
7. Help them to manage their time, money and energy.
8. Teach them by forgiving, being kind when they make mistakes.
9. Make them feel that they are capable, useful, resourceful for the family and the society.
10. Teach them the facts of life.
11. Look after their friends and interact with them, their parents.
12. Make mealtime a pleasurable occasion. Discuss what really matters.
13. Inspire them to watch news, read newspapers, good books, good magazines, and get these for them.
14. Go for outings and share their moments, being friendly.
15. Know their teachers and interact with them.
16. Visit the school/college – periodically.

17. Limit their gossiping/chatting/TV viewing.

18. Make them self-reliant and never do the things that they should and they can do.

19. Never accept anything bad – even in moderate form.

20. Don't defend them always – blaming others. Examine before you take any action.

21. Create a desire in them to aim high, think big and work hard to achieve it.

22. Instil a dream and help them to strive for it.

23. Study their weakness and strength – and advise accordingly.

24. Help them, cooperate with them, to be better students for a brighter career.

25. Make them God-fearing, loving, caring human beings to live for themselves, for family, for nation.

Parents Please!

1. What is your strength?

_____

_____

_____

2. What is your weakness?

_____

_____

_____

3. Do you have good friends? What do you usually talk when you meet them?

_____

_____

_____

4. What do you think of our country?

_____

_____

5. What do you think of the next generation?

_____

_____

6. Do you believe that the young minds, including your child, can build a better nation?

_____

_____

7. Do you feel that you should encourage your child, other children and young minds, for a better and brighter tomorrow?

_____

_____

8. Do you think you can play a major or even a little role to present a new generation after some years, and how?

_____

_____

_____

9. Do you think children should understand and realise what they need to do at an early stage of their life?

_____

_____

10. Do you believe in the universal power of God? Do you believe it is helpful and supportive for every-one?

_____

_____

Your child - young mind - your asset

Evaluate him:

1. How do you feel of him?

_____

2. What is his strength? What is good in him?

_____

_____

3. What is his weakness? What is wrong in him?

_____

_____

4. What can you do to develop his strength and eradicate his weakness?

_____

5. How do you want to see him after:
    i.   Three years –
    ii. Five years –
    iii. Ten years –

6. Do you believe that your child can grow to be a good human being, an able scientist, a technocrat, an inventor or a great man?

_____

7. Do you find anything significant in your child, something you are really proud of?

_____

8. Do you find anything in your child you are really embarrassed about?

_____

_____

9. Can you believe that:

You can resolve to be little better and set an example to inspire, motivate, encourage not only your child, but children of his generation?

_____

_____

10. Can you dare to instil a dream in your child and strive hard on your part to make him fulfil it for the benefit of our countrymen?

_____

_____

Your Decision

For your child, for your family, for our nation
Write ten statements what you decide to do.

_____

_____

_____

_____

_____

_____

_____

_____

_____

_____

Gift your child – this page.
Make him read it, and feel PROUD OF YOU.

ॐ ☙

Educators Please!!!

A teacher affects eternity,
he can never tell where his influence ends.
—*Henry Adams*

Teachers are second parents. They complete the term of education in different periods of the life of young minds. Next to home, the young minds spend most of their time in this environment. Teachers are role models. They are responsible to impart education, provide knowledge and wisdom. They are the source of inspiration to do something new, something significant, something innovative – on the part of the growing mass of young minds. Teachers should help them to find their purpose inlife and strive hard to fulfil by – *the power that is knowledge, when put to use.* Teachership is not a position – but an action being pure, honest and decent. Our future depends on the young minds, and the future of the young minds depends upon the teachers, be it in schools, in colleges or in universities. Teachers should understand the ability of these young minds and equip them for a brilliant career and magnificent achievement.

> *There is something that is finer far,*
> *something rarer than ability.*
> *It is the ability to recognise ability.*
> —*Elbert Hubbard*

Individual ability, when taken care of, arouses the interest of the child to learn in the midst of joy and happiness. Teachers should teach the value of education, and allow them to stand tall in the crowd. Teachers should encourage, inspire the children to learn and know, to grow and glow – **dim to dull, dull to bright, bright to brilliant** – to brighten the future of a nation. They should equip the children for living a life of happiness and success for self and society. They should teach the young minds to value their character and refine their manner, to practice honesty, integrity and courage. They should instil the pride of self-esteem and help them develop the strength to handle the problems of life and of nation. They should compliment every child every moment, as they play a major role in shaping, forming and moulding the living clay.

> *I took a piece of plastic clay,*
> *and idly fashioned it one day,*
> *and as my fingers pressed it still,*
> *it moved and yielded to my will.*
> *I came again, when days were passed,*
> *the bit of clay was hard at last,*
> *the form I gave it, still it bore,*
> *but I could change that form no more.*
> *I took a piece of living clay,*
> *and gently formed it day after day,*
> *and moulded it with power and art,*
> *a young child's soft and yielding heart.*

I came again when years were gone,
it was a man I looked upon,
he still that early impress bore,
but I could change that form no more.

—*Anonymous*

Teachers leave the mark, leave the impressions on the young minds which time can never rub out. They have the future of the nation in their hands. Thus, they should act as a fellow traveller, quenching the need of the students. They should instil and infuse dreams and help the students to grow in body, soul and mind. They should make hard things easy and change the repulsive texts into attractive reading. *Teachers should accept that they are doing a great job to change even the course of a nation.* Life changes day by day and they should update, adapt and improve their minds to *move the history, develop the science, and teach the art of living.* Prioritising some and neglecting others is not a healthy sign for teachers. They should teach the young minds in a way essential to find the right process for the right product, to take care of the means to get better ends. They should prove that the roots of education are bitter, but the fruit is always sweet.

Teaching, not only to store in memory but to **think** for using it, not merely for earning a livelihood but also for living, not merely for temporary benefit but also for times to come, is the real value of education. Using positive words, positive statements, teachers can create a positive attitude among the young minds to enjoy the life of peace and progress.

The tendency of the young minds is to be noticed, to feel significant, important. Teachers should take effort to suit the feelings of children by being considerate. They must do the things that children really need and not what pleases them. Discipline is the main thing in achieving greater results. When children are troubled with overcrowded classrooms or lack of facilities due to lack of funds, they lose their chance to develop their full potential. It is their loss, so also the loss of the community. They either struggle hard to survive or lose their purpose, in life. In addition to thinking on solutions, the best thing is to inspire and encourage them, which can make a permanent impact to work hard persistently, even in the environment of insufficiency.

A teacher who is attempting to teach without inspiring the pupil with a desire to learn is hammering on a cold iron.
—Horace Mann

Make the children creative, innovative, inventive – inspire and improve their skill. Enhance their knowledge. Give them fun and pleasure through studies. Help them imagine, visualise, by exploring the probabilities. Give them the role models. Ask them, interact with them, guide them. Explain the power of decision and determination. *Teach them to make decision, to take action which can transform our nation.*

Make them well-equipped, to face life. Let them be assets for family and society.

Once they get ready to accumulate more and more in their knowledge bank, it will surely help them to expand their thinking, empower their belief, changing their attitude and teaching them the philosophy of life and living.

Any satisfactory system of education should aim at a balanced growth of the individual and insist on both knowledge and wisdom.
It should not only train the intellect but bring grace into the heart of man.
Wisdom is more easily gained through study of literature, philosophy and religion.
If we do not have a general philosophy or attitude of life, our minds will be confused, and we will suffer from greed, anxiety and defection.
Mental slums are more dangerous to mankind than material slums.

—Dr. S. Radhakrishnan

Teachers Please!

Your responsibility – for young minds

1. Raise their spiritual and moral standard.
2. Be caring – know everyone, their background, their interest, their need, their weakness, their strength.
3. Interact with each one, with understanding and consideration.
4. Discuss social, national problems and instil greater thoughts.
5. Make them curious, enthusiastic, brave, decent, competent, confident.
6. Give value-based examples while teaching.
7. Update yourself, learn more and more to expand your knowledge bank.
8. Make your voice clear, language audible, mannerism decent, and make the class interactive.
9. Take classes being well prepared, well informed with teaching aids.
10. Present properly and involve everyone, to imagine, realise and memorise.
11. Discuss varied questions, various answers.
12. Maintain discipline and practice integrity.

Favourite Teacher/Tutor/Counsellor. Please!

1. What is your strength?

   _____

2. What is your weakness?

   _____

3. Where do you need improvement?
   Personally:

   _____

   Professionally:

   _____

4. Can you evaluate your performance – according to the students?

   _____

5. Do you refer to books to present your teaching in a better way?

   _____

6. Are you a learner?

   _____

7. Do you read books, magazines, newspapers regularly, to understand the current affairs?

   _____

8. Do you read biographies or autobiographies of great people?

   _____

9. Do you try to improve yourself personally and professionally?

_____

10. Do you enjoy life and feel proud to be a teacher?

_____

11. Do you teach with examples?

_____

12. Do you encourage the young minds for a better and greater nation?

_____

Write ten statements, on the _concerned young mind,_ – suggest, guide, advise him, as you know, feel and realise his activities.

_____

_____

_____

_____

_____

_____

_____

_____

_____

_____

Make him read and THANK, AND REVERE YOU.

છ્ર ભ્ર

Manage your Mind

It is not good enough to have a good mind,
the main thing is to use it well.
—Rene Descartes

We ought to be more concerned about removing
wrong thoughts from the mind than about tumours and
abscesses from the body.
—Epictetus

Mind rules the body – is the most fundamental
fact which we know about the process of life.
—Dr. Franz Alexander

Our mind rules our body. It is like – we are minds to which body is attached. The body functions according to the directions of the mind. Mind influences inside, to get the actions outside – by the body. We come across different events, meet different people, confront different problems and that is the way our mind is influenced by numerous societal practices, to build us as individuals. We think, we believe, we act, we grow, according to the input given to our mind. Our physiological and psychological development forms our personalities. Our physical stature, our composition may be a matter of heredity, or dependent on the molecular structure of genes located in the chromosomes, but our psychological norms – come from our environment – our family, our friends, our mates, our community, our society, and from different situations, events, cirumstances that we come across in our day to day life.

Our thinking, our attitude, our emotion – is thoroughly moulded and exhibited as we learn all the years from all these sources. The mind regulates, influences, controls, guides our body. We act and interact, we act and react – according to the direction of our mind. We read, we learn, we store in our mind. We retrieve, we recall, we remember and express what we have stored. The most important function of our mind is to **THINK.**

We human beings are essentially thinking machines. We think of our experiences, we think of our acceptances, we think of our situations. We decide, we conclude, we infer by our thinking. We organise, we associate, we evaluate in our thinking. Our life has been controlled by our thoughts based on what we listen, what we see, what we accept and *what we speak to ourselves.* Thoughts have tremendous power. We are the result of our thoughts. We hope, anticipate and expect in our thinking. We imagine,visualise, picturise favourable or unfavourable outcome in our thinking. Our desire, in form of thought, later creates the fact.

We perform actions according to our thought. We have travelled from the pre-historic era with the power of thought. The thought of hunger leads to get food. The thought of poverty leads us to be rich. The thought of problems leads us to get solutions. The magnificent skyscraper, or a button of a shirt came first in the form of *thought*.

Inventions, discoveries, progress, advancement, health, wealth are the result of **thought by the people, who thought and who believed.**

They are the thinkers.

All great people are great thinkers. They realise the power of thought. They believe in the power of thought.

The universe is transformation;
Our life is what our thoughts make it.
—Marcus Aurelius

The ancestor of every action is a thought.
All thoughts tend to convert themselves into action.
A man is so, what he thinks all day long.
—Ralph Waldo Emerson

Men often become, what they believe.
—Mahatma Gandhi

Dynamic thought or belief helps
create the actual fact.
—William James

We lift ourselves by our thoughts;
We climb upon our vision of ourselves.
—Orisson Swett Marden

To think, is to live.
—*Marcus Tullius Cicero*

I think, therefore I am.
—*Rene Descartes*

Thought is the light of the world and the chief glory of man.
—*Bertrand Russell*

Think big and your deeds will grow,
Think small and you will fall behind,
Think that you CAN and you WILL,
It is all in the state of mind.
—*Anonymous*

All that a man achieves is the direct result of his own thoughts. A man can only rise, conquer and achieve by lifting up his thoughts. He can only remain weak and abject and miserable by refusing to lift up his thoughts.
—*James Allen*

All impulses of thought have a tendency to clothe themselves in their physical equivalent.
—*Napoleon Hill*

As a man thinketh in his heart, so is he.
—*Proverb by King Solomon*

Thinking is in the mind but accepting in the heart is believing. As a man thinks and accepts or believes himself, so he is. As a family thinks and believes, so it is. As a community thinks and believes, so it is. As the members of our nation think and believe, so we are, so is our nation. If we think and believe we are great, then so are we. **If we think and believe we can be greater with great achievements, great accomplishments, great performances, so can we.**

We may think or not, it is up to us, because when we think, we get problems, when we don't think, we make excuses, but if we think **we can,** we can, if we think **we can't,** we can't.

If we think we are sure to achieve – our thoughts are translated into action to succeed. If we think we may fail, we increase the chance of failing.

All that we are is the result of what we have thought.
—*Buddha*

What we think today is important to decide what shall we be tomorrow.

Yad bhavam, Tad bhavathi.
(You become, what you think)

Our miserable thoughts make us miserable. Our fearful thoughts make us fearful. Our sickly thoughts make us sick. Our failure thoughts make us fail. Our success thoughts help us succeed.

To be happy – not to think up sorrow.

To be prosperous – not to think up poverty.

To be successful – not to think up failure.

Think up refers to consider, to plan, to conceive, to compose in mind, forming ideas, understanding the pros and cons and reaching the conclusion, and not rearranging the prejudices, superstitions and beliefs which might prompt just the opposite, because whatever we have thought or whatever we think will be converted into a fact. Our dominating thoughts – habitual or intentional, planned or unplanned – associate similar thoughts in the imagination, and allow us to think upon, more and more, deeper and deeper, stronger and stronger, that gradually force us to act.

When we think, feel and accept failure we fail, as our actions are regulated to make us fail. When we think, feel and accept success we succeed, as our actions are regulated to make us succeed. Any thought which is stronger and deeper passes into our subconscious mind, helps it to convert into a physical form. That is the power of our subconscious mind.

Basing on functions, attributes and power, we can differentiate our mind as two distinctive parts – the surface or the conscious mind and the deeper or the subconscious mind.

Our conscious mind teaches us through the help of our sense organs or sensory tools – our eyes, ears, tongue, nose and skin.

Our subconscious mind looks after our internal functions. It takes care of heartbeat, controls blood circulation, regulates our digestion, looks after assimilation, guides elimination, never sleeps and functions continuously, even to see that our nails and hair grow.

Our subconscious mind stores what we learn, i.e., the names, facts, events, experiences, situations, circumstances, conditions, happenings, instances, and reminds us when and what we try to recall from it.

Our subconscious mind is upward, lifeward, God-ward. It is the creative mind, and the connecting link between our finite mind and the infinite universal intelligence.

When we think, we use our conscious mind and what we think regularly, habitually, strongly, sinks down into our subconscious mind which creates the fact according to our thought, associating all the information, all the knowledge from inside and from outside, giving us the power, the energy and the wisdom.

Habits are formed by continuous practice in the conscious mind, till it is accepted by our subconscious mind. We learn to ride a bike or type on a typewriter by our conscious mind, till our subconscious mind is trained.

A salesman in a medicine store looks about left and right and finds the exact medicine to sell, even while talking to a customer or intermittently watching the India-Sri Lanka One-Day match.

We live on our habits, our conditioning, our training to the subconscious mind, which makes things happen, unless and until our conscious actions do not obstruct or block its power.

> *The great discovery of the nineteenth century was*
> *not in the realm of physical science. The greatest*
> *discovery was the power of the subconscious touched*
> *by faith. In every human being is that limitless reservoir*
> *of power which can overcome any problem in the world.*
> —**William James**

The subconscious mind, backed by faith, has astonishing power. It can create the fact, according to our thought, only when we suggest it. Our subconscious mind listens to repeated suggestions. We are controlled, guided and monitored by our own suggestions to ourselves, which are not exactly ours but what we learn from others. According to our suggestions, the subconscious accepts the mental pictures and stores it to help us act, and get it to happen, irrespective of it being useful or harmful, good or bad, bringing failure or success for us. Thus, what we are is because of our thought, strong thought, regular thought and the most dominating thought.

If we regularly think of bitterness, resentment, frustration, failure, sickness, what do we get? If we regularly think of health, success, happiness, what do we get? God's law is Nature's law, Nature's law is the law of belief. The atmosphere is filled with good and evil, health and sickness, poverty and prosperity, peace and unrest. God's answer is abundance and fulfilment, health and happiness.

When we believe in Him, when we pray to Him, when we think success and happiness, it can create the fact of happiness, success and prosperity, by providing us the ideas, intuitions, hunches to accept and work on.

But our conscious action, thought, emotion, filled with disbelief and doubt, resists the power of universal intelligence and restricts the flow of inexhaustible energy from the universal power.

Hence, we fail to accept that *we can,* or *we can with the help of God,* or *we can with the help of the universal power.*

Most of the time our thinking is really, in fact practically done by our parents, society, newspaper, television, media, environment and other resourceful factors, who think for us. We think, as they think.

We learn, we grow, we habituate, we are programmed, trained and conditioned according to them and never on our own.

To change the fact we need to change the thought. To get success we need to think up success.

When we think success, we proceed towards success. When we think failure, we proceed towards failure. Thinking on negative terms gets negative result. Thinking on positive terms helps to get positive results. Our thought process can be detected, can be controlled, can be guarded if it is negative, and can be replaced, erased and *substituted* by a strong positive thought.

The achievers in the world are great positive thinkers for themselves, for others. They believe in the power of God as they know, realise and believe in the universal power. They reject all the negative forces which stand as roadblocks to that power. Their strong thought, strong belief outwits, throw off all the negative influences and with the *powerful positive thought, they achieve even what the world calls impossible.*

They do not expect the result overnight, neither doubt it nor withdraw from it. They never entertain the thought of pessimism nor allow it to form a *stronghold*. When a thought is instilled by someone, they cross-check it and with the power of positive statements, they counteract, to avoid depression. Sometimes, their mental storehouse does not get along, but they teach their subconscious and never opt the way for failure by accepting the negative thoughts in the form of words. Their positive words trigger to form positive thought and take them a long way accelerating, enlivening, enriching, enacting them with the power of faith and hope.

SCAN – NEGATIVE MIND

We exhibit — Anxiety, Worry, Tension, Depression, Pessimism, Misery, Sorrow, Agony, Insomnia, Diseases, Insecurity, Suspicion, Confusion, Chaos, Destruction, Unhappiness, Indecision, Cynicism, to get..... **failure.**

Because, we act out of — Jealousy, Envy, Greed, Selfishness, Immodesty, Deceit, Pride, Bitterness, Anger, Fury, Intolerance, Frustration, Perversion, Hypocrisy, Rigidity, Cowardice, Impurity, Unjustness, Unrighteousness.

Because our thoughts are filled with.....
Fear, Doubt, Hate — Fear creates doubt, which leads to hate. Fear, doubt and hate, individually or collectively, create every way that take us towards failure.

SCAN – POSITIVE MIND

We exhibit — Happiness, Courage, Decision, Commitment, Enthusiasm, Optimism, Growth, Health, Friendship, Benevolence, Goodwill, Peace, Patience, Competence, Discipline, Persistence, to get..... **success.**

Because, we act out of — Anticipation, Understanding, Courage, Friendliness, Cheerfulness, Optimism, Cordiality, Orderliness, Purity, Justice, Holiness, Righteousness.

Because our thoughts are filled with......
Faith, Hope, Love — Faith creates hope, which leads to love. Faith, hope and love, individually or collectively, create every way that take us towards success.

When your thought is filled with fear, doubt, hate –
disbelief in your ability, you suggest your mind, which
ultimately takes the spirit to produce the fact, accordingly.
You don't act or even if you do act, you do not do it
wholeheartedly, confidently, with belief. When your thought
is filled with faith, hope and love – *belief* in your ability,
you suggest your mind, which helps to act whole-heartedly,
confidently to produce the fact.

A thought filled with faith, hope and love is the secret
of achieving miraculous, astonishing, impossible things
because these thoughts harmonise with the power of God
which supports, creates, helps and does everything to get
the positive fact, and that is **positive thinking.**

Positive thinking is not a matter of instance, neither
is it a matter of just *yes* or *no.* Positive thinking is a
process. A positive thinker produces positive attitude,
positive emotion, positive action, which ultimately leads
to get positive result.

You can easily understand, know, realise what
type of a thinker you are, what your thoughts are filled
with –

Fear, Doubt, Hate, **or**
Faith, Hope, Love.

You are responsible for your result, for your action,
for your emotion, for your attitude, for your thought,
nobody, but you because,

you are what you think you are,
you are what you believe you are......

Think Positive.... Manage your Mind to think Positive.

Your Emotions

*There can be no transforming of darkness into light
and of apathy into movement without emotion.*
                                                    —Carl Jung

Emotions are nothing but the intense feelings which
are directed at someone or something. When it is less
intense it is termed as 'mood' and when it is stronger and
greater, in a combined form, it is termed as 'affect'. By
emotions we generally mean feelings, like happiness,
anger or fear. A positive state of mind exhibits positive
emotions like being happy, joyful, hopeful, loving and
peaceful. A negative state of mind exhibits being envious,
fearful, jealous, angry.

We usually forget if anyone compliments us, but we
remember if anyone laughs at us because of our negative
conditioning, programming, training. We recall all the
instances of similar kind and obviously, our subconcious
mind, if it has got a storehouse of such, opens up the file
to remind everything of that sort that we have learned,
throughout. Thus negative feelings, negative emotions,
seem stronger than positive emotions. We feel sad, we get
angry, we scold, we criticise according to our negative
input which strengthens our feelings. Emotions are
sometimes aroused by perception. Perception is the
information that our mind gets with the help of our
sensory organs.

What we see, what we perceive, what we understand
– that we feel. It may be different from the fact, but we
feel, and our emotions are regulated so. What we see
generally depends on our motives, interests, experiences,

expectations and attitudes. *We see things as we are and not as they are* and our emotions are created according to our thought when we see the object.

Anger, fear, sadness, happiness, surprise, are different kinds of emotions. Our emotions may be useful or may be harmful, may be functional or may be dysfunctional, may be negative or may be positive.

Negative emotions destroy the sense of fairness and peacefulness. They also destroy creative imagination, hamper learning and prevent you from achieving.

Emotions may lift you up or pull you down. Therefore controlling the emotion is as much essential as learning. Emotions play a major role in achievement than even academic intelligence. Controlling, maintaining, balancing the emotion can be possible by thinking in positive terms.

Control your negative emotions.

Fear

For it is not death or hardship that is a fearful thing,
but the fear of hardship and death.

—*Epictetus*

Your fearful thoughts can attract troubles. They can upset you, weaken you and can make you mentally sick. Millions of people are afraid of different things, and are haunted by some or the other kind of fear. You must try to understand that fear is mental in nature. It is in your thought and you are the host of it.

Normal fear — to avoid an accident, to take precaution against disease is good. Normal fear protects us, sometimes it even motivates us. But fear in thought, in imagination – to be sick, to be poor, to fail, to be alone – can take its toll.

Fear creates anxiety, fear of not performing well, fear of not achieving the desired end, fear of not meeting the expectation, fear of not fulfilling the ambition, creates anxious thoughts of –

(i)   What shall happen to my future?

(ii) What shall I do next?

(iii) How can I do better?

(iv) How can I be perfect?

(v)   How can I impress others?

(vi) How can I avoid ridicule or criticism?

(vii) How can I be appreciated?

Anxiety is felt for different reasons. Anxiety is a primordial phenomenon, where there is premonition of loss or lack of something or someone. Anxiety, if not controlled, strengthens the fear. Gradually, thoughts filled with anxiety make a person depressed, stressful, failing to overcome the constraints and meet the demands, and affects physiologically, psychologically, behaviourally, making the outcome uncertain, losing self-control and confidence.

Fear creates a negative feeling. It observes the negative side of everything and finds all possible ways of failure. It procrastinates till the end, it makes excuses, confuses, creates doubt and keeps you in a state of indecision.

Fear paralyses with disbelief. It constantly poisons and distorts your feeling, your thought. Fear makes you vulnerable. Fear makes you hypersensitive. Fear seizes you. Fear makes you motionless, suspecting everything, everyone – in imagination, things which never even happen.

Research says that whatever we fear –

40% out of that never happens,

30% out of that is past

12% out of that is needless,

10% out of that is petty and small,

8% is real but **can be solved** or **can't.**

In fact, man is born with two types of fear – fear of loud noise and fear of falling. All other fears are learned or acquired behaviour which we learn from others, our environment, our belief system, our thoughts, our emotions, our attitude.

> *Nothing is so much to be feared as fear.*
> —*Henry David Thoreau*

Fear of failing is the greatest roadblock for any achievement. Most of the people remain mediocre as they fear they may fail, and that makes them powerless. They imagine obstacles, hindrances, setbacks. Even if they start, the feeling of fear dogs them when they are midway.

Fear hinders the creative thought, it suppresses the positive imaginative skill, it reduces the possibilities of taking chance, thus stops the decisions, actions and ventures which could have taken shape. It never allows the genuine ideas to come up. It kills the constructive, positive, productive thought and damages your personality.

Fear of failing stunts your mental growth because you fear to learn, to grow, to achieve, to succeed. Moreover, there are always fearful things for everyone in daily life, even if they be silly.

When you come across a fearful situation, what do you do?

(i)   Do you become reactive, to escape from such situation, being an escapist?

(ii) Do you become aggressive, to circumvent being egocentric?

(iii) Do you transfer the responsibility by blaming others, being defensive?

Fear seizes you, so overcome fear. Be courageous, face it bravely. Mend yourself and face the fear.

He has not learned the lesson of life who does not
every day surmount a fear.
Do the thing you fear, and death of fear is certain.
—Ralph Waldo Emerson

The cure for fear is faith and then..... action, otherwise fear will lead you to worry. Worry about studies, about career, about life......

Anxiety → fear → depression → worry.

Worry is like a galloping horse. It jumps, but goes nowhere. It keeps on going, but takes you nowhere. Many people suffer by being worried. Many people even die, being worried. Stop worrying. Nobody dies of work, but some do die of worrying. Worrying causes irritability, loses objectivity and favours insanity. Your fear takes to.... hate.... to....doubt. Control your fearful thought, anxiety, depression, worry. Control your negative emotion.

Anger

It is just one letter short than danger.

It is the most destructive emotion which creates havoc in the family, in the society, in the environment. Anger is short madness. Anger is the secondary response to frustration. Frustration causes anger which is triggered when you are hurt, and sparked when you fear. Injustice, partiality, unfair treatment prompts anger. Extreme form of discontent leads to anger. An angry man demonstrates all the energy – physical, emotional and spiritual – to disunite, disintegrate, deteriorate everything, which could have been used otherwise. The emotion of anger makes a person indecisive, reactive and destructive.

A quick-tempered man acts foolishly.

—Proverb

Anger destroys the self-image of a person. Anger harms the physical, emotional, spiritual condition of a person. Anger make a person lose control on himself.

When a man grows angry, his reason rides out.

—Thomas Fuller

Anger is manifested –

by an active explosion or by passive control.....

What is your choice?

It is very much human to get angry, but it is essential not to let the anger control you. Avoid getting angry **or** atleast control your anger, for passive release.

Steps to control your anger:

Step 1 – Are my actions hurting others.... hurting me?

Step 2 – How are my actions hurting others.... hurting me?

Step 3 – How can I feel, know, realise to control my anger?

Why do you get angry? Isn't it your response? Sometimes anxiety, worry, depression, pressure, tension, stress, make people get angry. It is said that any problem is just ten percent because of its nature and ninety percent because of our response towards it. *A thought of problem itself is the main reason of our problem.* So what is the real reason of your anger? Go to it. Go to its root. Find out the reason..... and control your response. Think up a solution without being angered/angry.

When you get angry, your physical condition is changed, according to your emotional condition – but by changing the physical condition also, you can control your emotional condition. So you can make your mind quiet by making your body quiet, simply by controlling your physical actions.

> *When angry, count ten before you speak,*
> *if very angry, a hundred.*
> —*Thomas Jefferson*

Control your anger. Control your negative emotion. Remember, anger harms you long before it harms another person.

Can you...

(i) destroy a letter, written in anger?

(ii) initiate for a reconciliation, to save a friendship?

(iii) consider helping your oldage grandpa or his contemporaries without bitterness?

Develop your emotional intelligence. Remember, it plays a major role in shaping you to build a better personality. Emotional intelligence describes your capability, your competence, your efficiency, to control your emotions, especially negative emotions. It also specifies how you feel and understand others' emotions.

Sometimes people with higher level of academic performance, even with better standard of general intelligence, perform poorly in professional life because they are emotionally unstable.

Think of your exam, your career, your life; think of your parents – their expectation, your teachers – their demands, your relatives – their concern, and your performance as a student, as a young man, as a man – depends on your emotional intelligence. Learn it today, it is very much **in need today, tomorrow,** and **forever.**

Fear, doubt, anxiety, depression, tension, stress.

Manage it – by controlling your negative emotions.

If you are hurt, if you have scored poorly, if you have failed in your attempts, if you have exams ahead, if you have not prepared well, if you are unjustly criticised, if you are undergoing family stress, if you are betrayed, if you are deceived, if you feel yourself unworthy to count your life..... if you have a strong feeling 'Life can never be better'..... if you feel yourself unfortunate..... **if you are stressful.........**

Manage your stress.

1. Take it easy:

Take it easy, what has happened has already happened. Don't try to run away. You have not done well. You are being insulted, your friends are showing ingratitude, you are troubled, you think up the future to be dark and dull. Don't worry. Don't spoil today for yesterday. Accept what you have done. Start thinking of a solution.

2. Control your emotion:

You feel sad, you get angry quickly, you are uncontrolled – emotionally. Check your action, check your feeling, check your thought. You can't instantly change your mind, but you can instantly control your action.

You can simply banish your fear, worry and thus various kinds of illness, by *controlling* your action and *changing* your thought.

3. Believe in God:

When you believe in God, and pray, you draw power to overcome the thought of anxiety, worry and depression to surmount the hardship. You can make Him your companion to guide you, counsel you, bless you mercifully – who can empower you, strengthen you and fill your mind with thoughts of faith, confidence and security to be happiest, healthiest and best. You can have a life of joy and satisfaction and can have peace in mind to start your day – calm and composed.

4. Develop self-confidence:

Worry, depression, failure often bring shame, even a sense of cowardice. Be courageous. Muster strength, develop confidence to comfort yourself. Motivate yourself. Believe in your capability and act with "I can do" attitude. Keep yourself busy. Be polite. Avoid aggression. Avoid self-condemnation. Help others. Forgive and forget. Eat healthy food. Exercise regularly. Think great. Work hard. Stay encouraged. Be refreshed.

Failing doesn't make you a failure, but staying there does. *Believe that a setback is a set-up for a comeback.* Yes..... **come back.**

5. Take up the responsibility:

Take the responsibility and never blame anyone. This will help you to understand your weakness, which you can improve on. Blaming others will never allow you to find your fault, rather it will act as a hindrance, to a proper solution. Decide to do. Decide to act. Learn from your experience. Take up the responsibility to find a solution.

6. Take a strong decision:

It is very much normal to be indecisive when there is anxiety, depression. But you must decide, building enough strength to overcome. Identify your problem. Often a serious and complex problem is nothing but the composition of various small problems. Break them into the simple – to solve them. Suppose, your performance is poor in your exam. See not only the subjects you have done badly, but also the lessons, the parts of the syllabus, where your performance is low, and decide to improve. Take the strong decision quickly without retreating or waiting. This will help you save your time and can encourage you to act quickly.

7. Be positive to develop and improve:

Your thought is translated into action. Have positive thought to do well. Make strategies to get busy. Give no time to worry. Lose yourself into action. Work and play. Strengthen your mind. Change your thought, learn to profit from your losses.

8. Visualise your success, your happiness, your betterness:

Recall your joyful moments. Get the mental pictures clearly. Then preplay the same happiness, fun and pleasure in the future, in the days to come. Think up, believe and imagine how you are succeeding. Store the mental picture to retrieve it often.

9. Relax and rest:

Don't be dim or dull. Forget for a while and laugh. Laugh and laugh. Laughing can balance your anxiety. If you can't laugh at yourself, people will laugh at you. Reject the bitter experience. Laugh, relax, listen to good music, see the funny things. Make it a habit to smile. Take a deep breath. Play a soothing tune. Plan a dinner. Make a call. Read a good book. Sleep well. Rest well.

10. Start working on solution:

Don't waste time by looking **long** at the door which is already closed, but try to see the door which is readily opened for you.

Be confident. Think and act, cheerfully. Start working for a solution to solve the problem. Prioritise your activities and maintain a regular, healthy schedule to perform required actions. Make a list and by the end of the day, watch your improvement – not only in studies or in career – *but see that you are getting better and better in every possible way.* Insulate your mind against remembering the hurting moments, failing moments. Keep it for the healing power of time. Take care of your future which can be bright and brilliant. Go ahead. Still there is time for you, opportunity for you, chance for you and your intelligent effort for you.

> *Don't waste life in doubts and fears,*
> *spend yourself on the work before you,*
> *well assured that the right performance of the hours'*
> *duties be the best preparation*
> *for the hours or ages that follow it.*
> —*Ralph Waldo Emerson*

Positive emotion:

Love

> *If you could only love enough, you could be*
> *the most powerful person in the world.*
>
> —*Emmet Fox*

If you believe in the most powerful positive emotion on the Earth, obviously you will be powerful. The more people you love, the more powerful you are.

Love can cure, love can repair, love can restore. Love can reform, love can transform. Love can brighten, love can enlighten. What love is?

> *Love is patient, Love is kind,*
> *Love is not jealous, Love is not boastful,*
> *Love is not arrogant, Love is not rude,*
> *Love doesn't insist on its own way.*
> *Love is not irritable, Love is not resentful,*
> *Love does not rejoice at wrong, but rejoices*
> *in the right,*
> *Love bears all things, believes all things,*
> *Hopes all things, endures all things.*
> *Love never fails.*
>
> —*New Testament*
> *(The Holy Bible)*

Love suffers long. It is long-tempered. It avoids quick retaliation, or immediate punishment. It does not allow to get angry, neither does it nourish the bitterness to be revengeful. It encourages kindness, avoids harshness. Love doesn't envy. Love does not take pride, rather believes in humility. It never blows its own horn at the cost of others. Love listens to others and understands their feelings. It is never rude to wound others, hurt others. Love never forces to get things its own way. Love does not create irritability. It is never provoked to be resentful. Love does not take pleasure when others fail, neither does it think evil for others. Love enjoys the right, believes the truth and depends on God. Love tolerates everything, takes all the burden without pride or irritation. It believes God through disappointments, disillusionment, depression. Love hopes all things for better, works for all to make better. It endures, perseveres, persists. It never fails.........

Some people define love as a temporary feeling, others feel that it is nothing but a physical relationship. Some feel it to be self-sacrifice. Love is a vast concept. It has different meanings for different people. But the love that is real love is accepting others, caring for others, saying and doing – **I am with you and for you.**

Love is powerful. Love gives and forgives. Love forgives and forgets. Love reduces friction to fraction. Love cleans. Love clears.

Love changes lives!

With love one can gain knowledge, find wisdom and can achieve greatness.

Love is a feeling being nice, kind and honest. Many people do not realise the power of love. They envy others, look at others through a microscope, but loving people look at others through a telescope. Love doesn't find fault but remedy. Faults become thick when love is thin. Loving people never judge others, criticise others, or hate others, but they love others.

> *If you judge people, you will have*
> *no time to love them.*
> —*Mother Teresa*

People do not love others because they are frightened to lose their self-interest. They sacrifice the sense of fairness only to satisfy their wounded ego. They work hard to maintain Self-(non?) deserving vanity. They practically torture themselves mentally and internally without loving and without being loved.

Without love, there is no consideration. Without love, there is retaliation, there is confrontation, there is confusion, there is chaos and destruction. Without love, words sound like noise. Human beings behave like other animals. Without love, a relationship becomes self-centred, anger is routinely exhibited, loss is thoroughly invited.

Moral decline, self-interest, pride, personal pleasure, excessive desire for wealth, materialism, etc, threatens the power of love in the world.

> *The world doesn't need any more mountains to climb*
> *or rivers to cross. What the world needs now is love,*
> *sweet love, not just for some, but for every one.*
> —*Jackie Deshannon*

For everybody there is the need of love. *The love which is sacrificing, which is performing, which is doing others what you need yourself to be done.* Some people confuse 'lust' with love. They say true love or false love, genuine love or superficial love. Love is love, not lust. Lust kills life, love gives life.

Love is pure, love is eternal, love is holy.

Love is not the lust of eye, neither lust of flesh. Some young minds understand and derive the definition of love from the river of fire which can burn their future, and their life, before they become men on earth.

A youth boiling with hormones will wonder why he should not give full freedom to his sexual desires. If he is unchecked by customs, morals and laws, he may ruin his life before he matures sufficiently to understand that sex is a river of fire that must be banked and cooled by a hundred restraints, if it is not to consume in chaos both the individual and the group.

—Will Durant

It is better for you to use your power, and energy, to achieve your worthy end.

Don't misuse the power of the most positive emotion on the Earth.

Love yourself.

Love your appearance, feel great. Love your body, never misuse it.

Love your soul, never embitter it. Love your conscience, never deceive it.

Love your work, find pleasure in it.

Love your career, love your future, love your life.

Love your parents, listen to them, don't take their love to be obvious.

Love your teachers, respect them, don't take their love as their job.

Love your God, honour Him, don't take His love as your right.

Love the animals, love the plants, love Nature, love the universe.

Love your friends, love your relations, love your neighbour, love the fellow human being, love the enemy, turn him into a friend....

Respect others, respect yourself. If you respect and love yourself, you can love and respect others. You can give what you have and not more than that. Your self-esteem is nothing but the respect you feel for yourself. If you are concerned about yourself, (don't take it as being selfish, at the cost of others) you can never hate others, because if you hate others, they will hate you and you can never be happy with yourself, because *"Love begets love. Hate begets hate."*

Love others, they will love you; care for others, they will care for you; respect others, they will respect you. It is not your intelligence but love that can work wonders. "People won't care how much you know, until they see how much you care."

If you are a failure in relationship, anywhere, don't worry. Instead of feeling and being insecure, lonely, despairing or angry, forgive and forget. Failure in a relationship is a matter of attitude, never feel regret for it. Your career and your life are much more important than that!

In the family, in your sphere, in any environment, do the following to express your love. Say it and show it.

(i) Understand others.

(ii) Be attentive to others.

(iii) Fulfil your promise.

(iv) Expect and express clearly what you need.

(v) Maintain integrity and chastity.

(vi) Admit quickly, if you are at fault.

(vii) Apologise readily, if you are apologetic.

The love of God and parents is sometimes tough, sometimes tender, don't misundersand them.

Talk to everybody, lovingly. Be lovable, maintain, protect and preserve PEACE on Earth by being a lovable creature.

Love and leave anger,
Work and leave hunger,
Laugh and live longer.

—*Anonymous*

You can do it for yourself

1. Do you have **faith** in yourself, to **hope** something good, something beautiful, something great, to achieve for the people, whom you **love**?

2. Do you have faith you can overcome imaginary fear?

3. Do you have faith you can control your anger?

4. Do you have faith you can control your feelings, when you face setbacks? Can you still keep hope and motivate your inner self?

5. Do you have faith you can understand others, their feelings?

6. Do you have faith you can manage your mind well?

7. Visualise your action/reaction in the following situations:
   — your mother calls you repeatedly for lunch, when you are busy preparing notes and not willing to divert.

— your friend is continuing his talk, over phone, and you don't want your time to be wasted.

— you are waiting for a bus, it arrived late, but there is no place for you.

— your teacher is displeased because of your dress code.

— you have left your bag, (books, notebooks) in a shoe store and returned home, with a pair of new shoes.... only to be scolded.

— your exams are approaching but your friends are convincing you to join them for a movie.

— you have not eaten well at home, you have money to eat outside, but you can't find time because of your exam schedule.

— you get unwanted calls on your cellular phone.

— you are in a hurry so you requested your uncle to drop you, but your uncle said 'No'.

— your parents are encouraging you, but your sister, along with your neighbour, is criticising you.

ಐ ಚ

Develop your Attitude

Attitude is everything. Make sure to have a good,
positive, productive attitude now and onwards...
if you really want to build a better you.
You can do much better in your career, in your life,
by simply changing your attitude.
Your success or failure
depends mostly on your mental attitude,
than your mental capacity.

Your attitude is your mental state which influences your response to all objects, situations and the people around you. That makes it the combination of your thinking, your emotion and your way of viewing events and circumstances. It reflects what you think, what you believe, what you feel and how you respond to things, that occur in your day to day life. *How you respond determines how you act and that determines what you get.*

When you find and feel the food for you is delicious, you even rush to kitchen to taste it. On the other hand, if you don't feel so, you do not do so. Your feeling for food determines your action of taking food.

When your teacher feels he is building a new generation, he works consciously and cautiously, but if he feels he is working for a salary only, his performance becomes poorer.

When one feels the task is worth rewarding or worth doing, he does it tenaciously, if not, he doesn't start it at all or even if he starts, leaves it midway.

When you feel that your studies, your efforts are important and essential for your career, for your life, **or** your performance is a requirement or expectation of your family, **or** a duty for your nation **or else**, when you feel to be an achiever – and believe that you can be a great asset to the family or the nation, you develop positive attitude and act enthusiastically, to reach the top.

But when you feel that you are for fun and pleasure only, you can take time to think, **or** you need not be serious about your career, **or** you are heading towards unemployment or you believe you can do everything later, you act accordingly. Your action is determined by your attitude, which is based on your informational, emotional, behavioural feedback from your mental storehouse, which may be habitual, but not permanent. *Performance of an individual depends more on mental attitude than mental capacity.*

Life is ten percent what happens to you and ninety percent how you react (feel) to it.

Your feelings, your attitude can be changed, and thus your action – which ultimately decides your result.

It is because of our attitude – we find the work funfilled, rewarding **or** drudgery.

It is because of our attitude – we find something impossible or possible.

It is because of our attitude – we are mediocre or great.

It is only with a positive and productive attitude – we can be greater, as a nation.

The nation's progress depends on the performance of every individual, and the peformance and individual action – is determined by feeling, by response, by attitude.

By changing the attitude, we can control and manage our thinking, our emotion, to make it positive, productive, which would bring the positive result.

As long as we think negative, we feel we can't be prosperous, we can't excel, we can't invent, we can't discover, we can't be advanced or developed..... to be greater..... so long as we can't.

By being positive, we can have positive attitude to change the situation, the circumstances and act to have a better personal and national living.

The greatest discovery of my generation is
that human beings can alter their living
by altering their attitudes of mind.
—*William James*

Attitude exhibits responses. Negative attitude gives negative responses, positive attitude gives positive responses. By default, we are mostly negative thinkers with negative attitude... to exhibit negative responses, and obviously get negative results – which seizes our performance, advancement, or fails to find solution to our problems, or retards, slows down the process of development, as a whole, to be greater.

Often, we think, discuss a lot about global warming, depletion of ozone layer, irregularity in climatic condition, rainfall, erosion of soil in flood, decrease in the yield, industrial and vehicular pollution, air, water, noise pollution...... pollution...... pollution......

We think.... discuss.... finally blame on this, and that.... (including ourselves!). Our discussion finally reaches to throw responsibility on others. We know that if anything can be done for this global problem, then it is **afforestation** first.

But, what is our attitude? We react, and we blame as we think, believe and feel, that it should be done by *some* of the people *only*. A person with positive attitude may discuss the problems, but it is not his reaction, rather concern. He realises deep in his heart that plants are essential for his living. An acre of trees produces four tons of oxygen. Plants are essential to absorb chemical pollutants, they help to reduce the noise level, they help in conservation of soil, they help in rainfall, they help get better climate, check global warming and are highly useful for him. So he is concerned, to think.

> *When people cease to complain,*
> *they begin to think.*
> —*Napoleon Bonaparte*

He stops complaining and takes the responsibility to think positive, and develops a positive attitude, plans for planting and becomes a part of the planting community. *Now, just imagine, even if one percent of the Indian mass get the same attitude to plant a tree in a year, we can get more than one crore new plants every year, apart from the departmental responsibility.*

Now, please don't visualise, calculate a variety of problems to say that it is impossible.....

Do you think planting a single tree, somewhere, some day in a year, for anyone, is impossible? Don't we have the time, money and energy for the manufacturers of **oxygen**? But it is our attitude that needs to change.

The same attitude prevails among some of the parents. For the younger children in their early school years, some of the parents blame teachers, some of the teachers blame parents, others blame both of them. *What do we need to be concerned to build* – houses, bungalows or the people to live inside?

It is true, it is real, that every individual is assigned a particular job. That is right, absolutely right, but is it not a fact that everyone can think a **little more, a little extra, a little beyond**, if the situation demands?

Now, who feels the demands of the situation?

Yes, of course there are many who feel, but do we feel or do we lament?

> *Don't lament that the times are bad,*
> *rather ask yourself what you can do*
> *to make them better.*
> *—Thomas Carlyle*

Now it depends on your feeling.

Your attitude – *towards your work, your family, your nation*, is what decides your action, your result, your performance.

When you think positive, your attitude is positive, you are optimistic with determination, with resolution and fixation of a worthy goal. Your facts may or may not allow you, but.....

Attitudes are more important than facts.
—*Dr. Karl Meninger*

Facts are facts, but sometimes based on our perception. We see what we find, and we find what we think. On the other hand – what we try to see, depends on what we feel to see and that is a matter of attitude.

Very recently, I met a gentleman who had just solemnised the marriage of his son. When I found him pale, I enquired: "Sir, what is the reason?" He started the story of his son, his marriage and expressed his happiness over the whole event, and annoyance at his son. He nourished an idea about his daughter-in-law's negligence and focussed on just to say that.....

"Look, my son is changed, being biased by his wife (not daughter-in-law?) and did not even ask me how to spend the money (accumulated in the form of gift) and left for Delhi." I asked: "Why so?" Then he replied: "I had strongly opposed the gift from the in-laws, so also anything, and everything from anyone." He also said that almost everyone was scared to talk to him, in this regard.

I appreciated it and said: "It is really great, sir."

He realised everything but went on telling.....

"Still, I expected my son to ask me what to do."

I convinced him somehow to take it easy, and requested him to talk to his son.

Later on, upon enquiry, Mr. Gentleman found that it (the money) is in the custody of **his** wife... (his son had deposited it in his mother's account) which all in the family decided to keep as a secret, fearing this gentleman's anger, audacity or greatness, whatever so!

The attitude he had developed towards his daughter-in-law was not based on fact but his perception, his lasting belief, his personal evaluation.

We cannot change certain facts in life, but our attitude can accept them. Managing stress, coping with the unavoidable, one can get rid of worry, anxiety, even illness, by simply changing the attitude. One can accept, solve, manage problems with a positive mental attitude in a more better way. No problem is ever a problem, to stand permanently. Problems can be solved, can be managed. A man is hurt by the opinion himself (about him), and not of others. It is said, the thought of any problem is not even ten percent because of its nature, and ninety percent because of our response towards it.

We spend time, money and energy on little things, little matters, thinking over and over, again and again. We fail to accept rejection, we fail to accept criticism, we fail to accept correction. What is our attitude?

Whenever we think big, whenever we aim high, we find all the barriers in mind, but when we can burst the barriers in mind, we can burst the barriers in reality.

Many people fear to attempt, fail to succeed even if they think, because their attitude about the temporary defeat is simple – they consider it as a great failure!

Great things are achieved meeting innumerable defeats, overcoming uncountable obstacles, surmounting incalculable hurdles.

When our attitude is positive, our vision is positive, we focus on the goal, neglect the obstacles. When our attitude is negative, our vision is negative, we focus on obstacles, neglect the goal.

For every achievement there is work, for great achievement there is great work, for great work great feeling, great thought, **great attitude.** Most of the people live a life – they regret for the past and are anxious about the future, but instead of doing something, feeling something, thinking something – they complain in the present.

Problems, setbacks, troubles......

For you, for your family, for your nation.....

It doesn't matter what happens *to* you but what happens *in* you. What you do, how you respond, how you feel, what you think, completely depends on you. Change your thinking, change your attitude, change your life. If you think, if you believe, if your attitude is indomitable and winning, you can achieve anything and everything in life.

> *Our belief at the beginning of a doubtful*
> *undertaking is the only thing that*
> *ensures the successful outcome of our venture.*
> —*William James*

Attitude can move us to like our work. Attitude can strengthen us. Negative attitude makes us – **we aren't, we can't, we won't.** Attitude is more important than fact. With a positive attitude, we can dare to do different and difficult tasks.

Accept and believe in the power of thought, power of emotion, filled with faith, hope and love. Take charge of your attitude, to achieve, to accomplish.

While I was preparing this book, it was a regular affair to take feedback from my students, my friends, my colleagues, parents of young children, intellectuals, common people, anywhere and everywhere, anything and everything – whatever I found important, significant and useful.

One day, I was in discussion with another gentleman who just didn't like my efforts of spending so much of time for this, and didn't find my effort of worth, in terms of inspiring the minds of young children. As a matter of advice, he started telling me: "Why do you spend so much time, take so much effort? Who is going to read it and how do you expect to transform them with a mere book?"

His inner voice meant – 'whatever you write, whatever you say, whatever you do, it can do no good.'

During the preparation of this little piece of work, as there is a saying, I have taken all criticism as normal, as casual and appreciation as bonus, but that day, I opened my mouth when the talk went beyond me and reached my target readers, (young minds, for whom I was specially writing this book).

"Sir," I admitted humbly, "that I am not a renowned author, so far all right, I am not a leader or a reformer or a psychologist or a mind manager, but to put it very simply, I am a citizen of India and I have an experience of more than ten years with the young minds. I have seen them, their growth, their life, and studied them closely.

I have seen life in rural India, in urban area, in cities. Whatever I find from different sources has taught me a lot. I have seen young children soaring high, being in different fields, so also I have seen some children losing their career, losing life. I have learnt a little how Indians are excelling and how can they excel further. I believe everyone is definitely good at heart. I believe they should learn how to live a life at an early stage. I believe they can do great things if they are encouraged. I believe they can succeed to advance as a greater nation. They can make the country, better and greater.

I see them as inventors, as discoverers as scientists, achievers.

I suggest them to make role models of the great scientists, the great leaders, the great performers. I believe they can make enough food for everyone. They can check the global threat for pollution, for peace. They can use the solar power and the natural resources. They can recycle the wastes and can make it useful. They can find better ways of irrigation, to get a better yield. They can join the riverways like the roadways and the railways to solve the problems arising out of natural calamities. They can develop talent in Information Technology and make it useful for everything, for everybody.

They can research, they can create, they can build, they can grow, they can glow.

Yes, they can glow and I believe so.

That is the belief, the thought, behind my effort," I continued.

"India has a population of more than a hundred crores and has hundreds of problems that need to be solved to be a greater nation, if not today, then tomorrow.

As elders, we could not fulfil dreams, let us atleast instil dreams and I am sure this work will be definitely useful, for anyone and everyone. Rest of the things, I leave to God. I can no way believe that it won't be read, or can't be useful for them, for anyone.

That is my attitude towards my preparation.

Positive, Productive – I believe."

Now let me ask you: "How can you tell what they can't be, why do you put limitation at this stage when they have enough time, enough resources, though may not have enough favourable circumstances. I request you to be positive and instil positive thoughts."

Finally, I said to him: "Can you say your child can never be an industrialist, never be an inventor, never be great. How can you and why do you say so! Do you take effort to get, to expect what he can't, what he can never..... then why do you say so! Nobody takes effort to get what he cannot. If he wants it he must speak. **John Logie Baird** invented the television, and helped you to watch cricket matches, sitting here. **Thomas Edison** invented the electric bulb, and lighted the whole world. **Bill Gates** developed softwares, and brought the computers to almost very home. *Get one, like them. Get more, like them.*

The concern is not to have only the software engineers or the cricketers, but to have scientists, inventors, achievers, Nobel Prize winners in different fields. *When children abroad think of flying in cars, moving with robots and reaching Mars, what do we do with the 'minds' here?*

Say, what you need, **think**, what you need. **Believe** that, and you can get what you need. **Act** according to your need. **Overcome** the problems to get your need. **Persist** to get what you need and.................. **GET, what you NEED.** That is positive attitude," I concluded and left the place.

My dear youngminds!
I am explaining all these things,
for you and your attitude.

Your attitude is yours....... your thought is yours..... No one else can think for you. Think success. Associate yourself with success. Identify yourself with success. Visualise your success. Find your strength. Work hard to overcome – your weakness.

Winners evaluate themselves
in a positive manner and look
for their strengths as they work
to overcome their weaknesses.
—*Zig Ziglar*

Your weaknesses can be corrected, can be improved. Work on it. Have a positive attitude towards change. Change is a process. It may not be possible overnight. But decide to go ahead, to build a positive attitude. Replace all the negative thought by substituting a positive, productive thought. Recall your experience of success and think up success. Add knowledge day by day. Associate ideas. Build a thinking group – discuss, enlighten, learn from each other, about the problems, the issues, the phenomena. *You can have many more inventions. You can set up many more industries. You can settle many more problems. You can eradicate many more diseases. You can root out many more social evils. You can undertake many more projects.* Think positive. Think solution. Think progress. Think advancement.

Be optimistic, have positive expectancy. Don't be dull or bored. Correct your emotional conflicts, and settle all your inner forces in motion. Evaluate yourself, what you are today and probably what you will be tomorrow. When thinking changes – attitude changes, behaviour changes. Think healthy thoughts. Cast away, pull down, root out – the negative thoughts about yourself. Affirm yourself. Talk to yourself. Reprogram your mind. Believe that you have potential. Shackle your old habit of thinking. Believe in the power of God. Be courageous to endeavour for an unexpected, impossible task. Divine power is with you. *There are people who are achieving being in poverty. There are people who are achieving with physical deformity. There are people who are achieving without proper facility.*

What is their attitude? **Positive.** What they do have with them? Only the **positive attitude** to get the task done.

Make a good start everyday with a positive outlook, and live a life of happiness. Find your purpose, your goal.

Get motivated. Who is going *to be* motivated? **You.** Who is going *to* motivate?

You... yourself can motivate you.

What is motivation?

Motivation is taken from the Latin word *'motere'* which means, to take action. Motivated action is the result of strong belief, strong thought, which induces you to act, triggers you to move, drives you to reach your destination. Your feeling, your thought, your words to yourself can motivate you.

Your parents, your teachers, your counsellors may advise you, guide you, inspire you. They tell you what to do, how to do, but it ultimately depends on you, to think. They may accompany you, support you, guide you, but it finally depends on you, your belief, your attitude. You may like their words that may fascinate you, energise you, but it does not last long if you don't accept. When your negative thought reminds you, you forget their guidance, their inspiration, and you **go back to stay back**. Unless, you yourself motivate your 'own self' – nothing can help you. To motivate your own self – use affirmative words, positive sentences, every moment, every day, for your inner talk, inner conversation.

Take responsibility of your career. Once you take the responsibility, you will find the purpose and the direction, and the strength to move forward. You encourage yourself, you energise yourself, you drive yourself. Create a need, nurture a need, for achievement.

When you are motivated, you can intensify your goal, suggest your mind and can persist to reach your goal. Create a drive to excel. Teach your subconscious. Get the light to reveal the darkness. Don't be in the darkness and complain about it. Fearful obstacles are mental in nature. Break them, with Divine Power.

The human personality can be touched with Divine Power and thus greatness can be released from.
—*Ralph Waldo Emerson*

Pray to God. Get the Divine Power to accomplish great tasks. Work hard. Take more time.

Grow confidence, develop patience.

Think big. Aim high.

Change your thought, your attitude, your self-talk.

Have a positive attitude to succeed.

Think Success!!!

THINK SUCCESS!

Think success, don't think failure.
At work, and in your home, substitute
success thinking for failure thinking.
When you a face a difficult situation,
think "I will win," not "I will lose."
When you compete with someone, think
"I am equal to the best," not "I am outclassed."
When opportunity appears, think
"I can do it," never "I can't."
Let the master thought "I will succeed"
dominate your thinking.

                          —*Dr. David J. Schwartz*

                      ജ ൙

Your mental attitude is much more
important than your mental capacity,
which can bring progress, success and
happiness for you, for others.
Be positive. Have positive attitude.

Grow faith in yourself, keep hope for good.
Have love for all.

DREAM BIG, AIM HIGH
THINK SUCCESS, SEE PROGRESS

Refine your Friendship

Friendship is a sheltering tree. There is only one acid test to select friendship. A real friend is one, who warns against an impending danger, and of course, guides through troubles.
—Samuel Coleridge

*R*eal friends warn and guide through troubles. They share, they multiply the joys and divide the griefs. Friendship is a choice, also friendship is a blessing. Friendship matters a lot for you, for your success... or failure. Friendship – is the means to make your life easier, funfilled, exciting. Have friends – to grow, to learn, to warn, to achieve. Good friends, without self-interest are your assets. Being good you can be an asset to your friends. That is the beauty of friendship. True friends are like diamonds – rare and precious. Cultivate them, nurture, and develop them. Care for them, they will care for you.

Accept each other – even with imperfections, but take effort to excel. Consider their individuality – but without self-ego. Respect their opinion – but weigh it if they differ. Give each other – a space, not for dominance, but for improvement. Be ready to give them, receive from them. Be eager to help, be free to ask for help. Your advice should not be your noise or your complaint or your criticism – but constructive, exemplary and co-operative. Tell them you like them, encourage them to do better. Be happy with their talent and congratulate them when they succeed. Express yourself, your thought, your feelings but never hurt them. Love them. Believe them. Have good friends or make your friends – good.

> *Associate yourself with men of good quality if you esteem your own reputation, for it is better to be alone, than in bad company.*
> —*George Washington*

Never hate anyone, even if you don't like some of them. Likewise, all may not like you. Take it easy if you are not at fault, and if you are at fault, then listen to anybody and everybody, till you correct it.

To have a good relation, keep your love in action by speaking to each other, listening to each other, looking for the good in each other, appreciating each other, sharing with each other, enjoying with each other, wishing each other, reporting each other, working for each other, caring for each other, loving each other. Take humour – wherever you go, but not at the cost of others!

Find a remedy for everyone. When anyone is in trouble – be beside, stand beside, to lift the heavy load by being courteous, friendly, in language and in action, in head and in heart.

What is happening to your friend today, may happen to you tomorrow. Be sincere to help, or to try to help. Sincerity beings multifold blessings.

When troubles come your soul to try,
you love a friend who just stands by;
Perhaps there is nothing he can do,
the thing is strictly up to you;
For there are troubles all your own,
and paths the soul must tread alone,
times when love can't smooth the road,
nor friendship lift the heavy load.
But just to feel you have a friend,
who will stand by until the end,
whose sympathy through all endures,
whose warm handclasp is always yours,
it helps somehow to pull you through,
although there is nothing he can do
and so with fervent heart we say,
'God bless the friend who just stands by.'
—*Anonymous*

Friendship – during thick, during thin. A friend in need is a friend indeed. Sometimes, friends use unfair language when they seem to be controlled by negative emotions. They get angry. Bitterness, resentment takes the upper hand, and kills the friendship. They never realise that language pierces and wounds the heart.

Angry friendship is sometimes
as bad as calm enmity.
—*Edmund Burke*

Still, it is better to get heavy blows, to learn from your friends, than to have false kisses from others. If you find your friend at fault, don't hesitate to reprove but secretly, and be alert to praise him openly. Be careful about your friends who flatter you. They are hypocrites, with self-interest, self-ego, self-doubt. They are not true to themselves, let alone true to you. Before they deceive you, they deceive their own conscience.

Good Friends:

   (i)   Never encourage you for sin ----- being an instigator.

   (ii) Never stop you from taking good action ----- being fearful.

   (iii) Never reveal your secrets ----- being very smart.

   (iv) Never hesitate to feel good, tell good about you -- being hypocrite.

   (v)   Never leave you in distress ---- being selfish.

   (vi) Never criticise before others ---- being funful.

   (vii) Never fail to help in need ---- being escapist.

   Good friends – during your prosperity you remember them, during your adversity they remember you. You are there for them. They are here for you. They are with you and for you to guide you, help you and grow with you.

   Friendship can be a great strength or a terrible weakness. When your friends are good, talks are good, thoughts are good – it is perceived, considered, believed – as strength. If it is not so, it is weakness for you! Cultivate friendship. You can interact, you can exchange, you can discuss more and more, deeper and deeper, stronger and stronger, about your career, your studies, your life and what matters, to your life, their life and the life of the nation. Have good, benefiting, stimulating ideas to achieve success.

Small minds discuss people,
Average minds discuss events,
Great minds discuss ideas.

Discuss ideas. Enlarge your interests. Widen your vision. Improve your thought. Develop your attitude. Learn from your experiences. Enhance your knowledge. Make better life, for everyone. Try to do something newer with a strong belief that – **your friendship can last and will not be lost.......**

You can do it for yourself

1. What do you mostly discuss with your friends?

_____

2. How do you consider your friends?

_____

3. Evaluate yourself, the way your friends consider you?

_____

Write name and telephone no. of ten friends.

_____

_____

_____

_____

_____

_____

_____

_____

Find out – Who inspires you? Who encourages you? Who helps you? They are your assets.

Who discusses — the ideas? He is the great asset.

Do you discuss so? Then you are great!

၆၅ ၆၆

Learn your Manners

Manners are of more importance than laws.
Upon them, in a great measure, the laws depend.
The law can touch us here and there, now and then.
Manners are what vex or soothe, corrupt or purify,
exalt or debase, barbarise or refine, by a constant,
steady, uniform, insensible operation,
like that of the air we breathe in.
They give their whole form and colour to our lives.
According to their quality, they aid morals,
they supply them or they totally destroy them.
— *Edmund Burke*

*Y*our manner is your behaviour in a specified way. Your manner reveals you. Your good manners reveal that goodness of yours. Your manner consists of how you talk, how you walk, how you make things happen in and around you. It represents how you express and expose yourself to situations, objects, or persons by speaking, by acting. Learn to use the right voice at the right time. The pitch of your voice (tonality), the way of your modulation, the style of your presentation decides whether you are a well-mannered or ill-mannered 'YOU'. Your speech should command respect and not authority, express self-dignity and not ego, establish self-esteem and not vanity. Your sense of humour should not sound like criticism, nor should it bear any grudges. Your speech reveals your mental state. A happy, joyous, peaceful mind produces proper expression and well-articulated sweet words. On the other hand, an unhappy, restless mind produces heated conversation, even leads to a fight. Evil words, evil language, spoil mannerism – even at the right time, for the right objective. Learn to speak good words – being polite.

People watch your words and they see, love, and appreciate you. Who wants to be surrounded by a person full of bitterness and resentment, expressing criticism, complaint and argument all the time?

> As a vessel is known by the sound
> whether it is cracked or not,
> so men are proved by their speeches
> whether they be wise or foolish.
> —Demosthenes

Learn to use the right words at the right time. Learn to speak – when you should not be silent and learn to be silent – when you should not speak. It is better to slip with the foot, than to slip with the tongue.

When you talk – be accurate, be concise, be careful, be honest and be the master of your own words. Your eloquent quotient depends on saying what is necessary and knowing what is unnecessary.

Always use soft words, polite verses, decent speeches – it will be helpful to avoid – displeasure, discontent, disunity. Your tongue is the pen of your mind. Write good things with it.

To gossip is a fault; to libel is a crime;
to slander is a sin.

—Anonymous

Some talkative people commit all the above three. They simply fail to understand the feelings of others and create embarrassment and disappointment for those around. Never be so, also avoid people of that sort.

The movement of your hands, the style of your walking, the way of establishing your posture forms an essential part of your mannerism. Learn to settle yourself or move yourself in a way that is pleasing to others. Remember, your expression is your most important wearing. Your dress code also makes a great sense. **Ben Franklin** said: "Eat to please yourself, but dress to please others." Take care to be a man of good manners.

Like character, manners and knowledge make a man. Manners are the expression of your conduct. Your manners decide the people in favour of you, or against you. Sometimes little things, which are neglected considering little, are judged seriously, viewed seriously by the people. Take care not to hurt others. You can learn to be well-mannered with practice. When you possess good manners, you can have the rest of the things you aspire. Good manners give good returns as well. It is required to acquire the manner first, then you can find the path free to acquire the matter, next.

How much easier it is to acquire
the manner than the matter.
—Rabindra Nath Tagore

Anyone can inculcate good mannerism or develop good manners – by being good and being in good company. People with good mannerism do better in different situations than the people without good manners. Civilisation is advancement by the people who are good mannered. Fine manners act like a passport which can help you to reach anywhere. It allows you to get in and present yourself. It allows you to sit for a good conversation and exit graciously.

Good mannered people give respect to others, as they respect themselves. Being polite, they exhibit good mannerism. There are some people who feel quite natural, even in a state of impoliteness. It is sometimes ridiculous and funny, at other times painful and disgusting. Avoid being so.

Your manner is the product of your loyalty and nobility. Avoiding falsehood, injustice, violence, pride, hatred; by embracing love, benevolence, care, you can be well-mannered. Good morals, good values form good manners. Ill-sense, ill-nature, ill-temper are the signs of bad manners. Practise good manners and be good. As according to **Voltaire**: "You may not always oblige to everybody, but speak obligingly." Control your temper. Mind your body language and learn your manners.

You are responsible not only for what information you pass on, but also what impression you leave and with what intention. So, always be quick to listen, slow to speak, very slow to get angry. You can exhibit a lot of 'goodness' if you are not bothered at all by, who takes the credit.

You are the best judge for yourself. You are the best teacher for yourself, and you are the only one to change, learn, unlearn your manners. The only corner of the world you are sure to change is **your** mini universe and the components attached to. The only way is to control your deeds, words, which, in fact originate from your thoughts.

> *Be not careless in deeds, nor confused in words,*
> *nor rambling in thought.*
> *If not seemly, do it not,*
> *if not true, say it not.*
> *Blot out vain pomp, check impulse, quench appetite;*
> *keep reason under its control.*
>
> *—Marcus Aurelius*

You can do it for yourself

1. How do you address others?
   — Respectfully, naturally.
   • From the head and heart and not from the lips.
2. How do you express yourself?
   — Have a smiling face (most important wearing!)
   • Learn where you are not supposed to laugh.
3. How do you expose yourself?
   — Be dignified with proper self esteem. Meet your friends with nice words.
   • Use words that please you, but definitely others also.
4. How do you stand, sit?
   — Stand straight, sit smart.
   • Don't sit in a slouched way, don't shake your leg.
5. How do you see, when one talks to you?
   — See front to front, be attentive and careful.
   • Don't look here and there.
6. How do you move your hands, your fingers?
   — Decently move your hands, use the palm.
   • Avoid pointing the finger.
7. How do you talk?
   — Talk nicely, soothingly in a right kind of tonality.
   • Not indistinctly or rudely. Avoid whispering before elders.

8. How do you exit?

   — Wishing, smiling graciously.

9. Use right, good, powerful, positive words, as often as you can.

10. **Make your manner for cooperation and not for conflict.**

Check your manner –

i. When you are entering into your School/College.

ii. When you are paying the bill to the hawker.

iii. When you are visiting a friend's house.

iv. When you are going to play with your friends.

v. When you are spending time in a restaurant.

vi. When you are going in an auto rickshaw to a cinema.

vii. When you are standing before your uncle.

viii. When you are appearing for your exam.

ix. When you are writing your cheque book.

x. When you are bargaining in a dress store.

ॐ ॐ

Value your Character

*Character gives splendour to youth
and awe to wrinkled skin and gray hairs.*
—**Ralph Waldo Emerson**

*C*haracter is the reality of yourself. It is made up of your particular qualities, that make you different from others. It is the essence of your personality. It is your true strength of power and riches. It is your inner core what you know about yourself. Your character creates your condition, your circle, your circumstances. Your mental attitude is the determinant of your character, which is eventually exhibited as different actions, in different times of your daily life. Character is excelling in – doing good, believing good and thinking good. Character makes you either good or bad, pure or impure, holy or unholy, both in public and private life. Character is the central theme of your life. Character is what you think of yourself, what you know about yourself, and how you act, being yourself. Good character is the combination of all good traits. Value your character. It is the best motive power for yourself and for others.

Character is not attained easily. It is practised little by little, bit by bit. Character values principles, maintains ethics, uses conscience to stand firm, to meet the ends in daily life. It is the never-ending, continuous, maintenance of your behaviour, irrespective of your situations and circumstances. It is built within, by your virtuous actions. It is not inherited from your parents but grounded by your own endeavour. It is the totality of you, based on your attitude, at the time of joy or grief. It is what you are when no one but God is watching you. To be a man of character, you need to remedy your deficiencies.

> *Remedy your deficiencies, and your merits*
> *will take care of themselves.*
> *Every man has in him good and evil.*
> *His good is his valiant army,*
> *his evil is his corrupt commissariat;*
> *reform the commissariat and the army will do its duty.*
> —*Edward Bulwer-Lytton*

By being truthful and performing acts of humility, politeness, patience, justice, forgiveness, kindness, loyalty, charity, and sacrifice – you can form your untainted character. To develop character – you have to resist the temptations and consistently exert the discipline – to avoid weak spots. A little trace of weakness can mar the bright career of your life. Even the insignificant trifles of righteous actions matter, to form your character, which can help you to withstand – in the face of immorality. Fear of God is the foundation of character which starts when you are a child and continues till you die. Personal purity and truthful sense is far more important than your education, your knowledge.

What is education without character,
and what is character
without elementary personal purity?
Put all your knowledge, learning and scholarship
in one scale and the truth
and purity in the other and the latter will
by far outweigh the other.
Knowledge without character
is a power for evil only.
—*Mahatma Gandhi*

Emerson said: "Character is higher than intellect." To develop character is as much essential as knowledge, and which can be attained by vigorous and persistent action. To build your character, you have to hammer and forge yourself, consistently and persistently. Most of the people try to build reputation, instead of character.

Living wickedly in private and superficially in public life may bring reputation for a while, but in the long run it is devastating and bound to taint your character. The best character is to try to live a life as you appear to be.

The shortest and surest ways to live with honour
in the world, is to be in reality what we would
appear to be. All human virtues increase and
strengthen themselves by the practice
and experience of them.
—*Socrates*

Some people change when the circumstance changes, when the place changes. They contradict their position and reputation – according to the changes. Character doesn't change, reputation does.

A man of character – remains the same in the bustles and turmoils of life. He rises above the circumstances and takes great effort to keep his character – intact. It is only in the degeneration and degradation of character that moral values degenerate. People want happiness, pleasure – at the cost of character. But people with character – outwit the weak spots and live a life of honour and greatness.

Grow to be a man of honour and character. Abide by the moral principles and purity. Trust God, avoid bad, avoid evil. Be sure, be aware there may not be anybody, but God is watching you. Build your character. Keep your integrity firm. You can be a great asset to your family, your community and your nation.

*A great character, founded on the living rock of
principle, is in fact, not a solitary phenomenon,
to be at once perceived, limited and described.
It is a dispensation of providence,
designed to have not merely an immediate but
continuous, progressive and never-ending agency.
It survives the man who possessed it;
survives his age – perhaps his country, his language.*
—*Edward Everette Helle*

Be truthful. Never violate truth. Have a relaxed mind, to have understanding. Learn good, even from the enemy. Have a high sense of morals. Be kind, be considerate, be compassionate, be generous. Care for others, and share with others. Be empathetic, to feel what others might be feeling.

John F. Kennedy said: "Don't fix a blame for the past, but fix a course for the future." **Abraham Lincoln** said: "He has the right to criticise, who has the heart to help." **Henry Ford** said: "Don't find a fault, find a remedy."

Don't blame others, even if you are suffering. Let them reap the thorns, if they sow thorns. Be a peace lover – build bridges instead of walls.

We have flown in the air like birds and swam the sea like fishes, but have yet to learn the simple acts of walking on the Earth like brothers and sisters.
—Martin Luther King

Keep peace, at home, in your institution, with your elders, with your friends. Build a value-based character. Maintain integrity. Being upright, stand firm in your conviction of purity and act in a way as you say, to become a man of integrity. Keep patience. Be humble. Avoid ego.

Integrity without knowledge is weak and useless, knowledge without integrity is dangerous and dreadful.
—Samuel Johnson

Work hard to build yourself. If anything is wrong, always try to *mend* and never try to *mask* or else it is equal to cheating, deceiving.

Never compromise with your convictions, with your values, with your ethics – you may have a good umbrella, but you will lose the roof. Dishonesty can take you nowhere. Never rest till your good is better, and better is best.

I shall pass through the world but once, if therefore, there is any kindness I can show, or any good I can do, let me do it now, for I shall not pass through this way again.
—Anonymous

You can do it for yourself

How do you grow yourself?

Are you compassionate or egoistic?_____

Are you joyful or unhappy?_____

Are you forgiving or vindictive?_____

Are you humble or arrogant?_____

Are you patient or impatient?_____

Are you honest or dishonest?_____

Are you transparent or deceitful?_____

Are you truthful or a liar?_____

Are you peaceful or angry?_____

Are you planned or impulsive?_____

Are you generous or covetous?_____

Are you dignified or undignified?_____

The best man is he who most tries to perfect himself and the happiest man is he who most feels that he is perfecting himself.

—Socrates

Be best. Be happiest.

80 03

Be yourself, Know yourself

Make it your business to know yourself.
It is the most difficult lesson in the world.
—Miguel de Cervantes

*Y*ou have three identifications – what the Creator knows, what others know, and what you know about yourself. The inner core of your heart knows who are you and what are you – what stuff you are really made up of. It may or may not be the same as what people know about you, but successful people, better people don't make any difference in this regard and live a life without sheltering in hypocrisy. Still, there are people who deceive others – by making little acts of unworthiness, and justify their stand before others, by doing something else. In fact, they deceive their own selves. Wrong thing is the outcome of wrong thought in secrect – something others may not perceive instantly. When the thought grows – it becomes difficult to get rid, and finally exposes as an action. The best thing is to insulate, or to reject, or to reform at the level of thought.

> *Never suffer a thought to be harboured in your*
> *mind which you would not avow openly.*
> *When tempted to do anything in secret,*
> *ask yourself if you would do it in public.*
> *If you would not, be sure it is wrong.*
> *—Thomas Jefferson*

As we have learnt in the previous pages, by controlling the mind you can habituate yourself for good thoughts and good actions. The first and foremost thing is to control the mind, to have a controlled body for any action.

Superior people control their body and mind and don't establish any difference before public or in private, and being transparent, live without any hidden traits. It is only when one realises, feels, evaluates oneself, that one understands what he really is. Thus the requirement to reform, improve, energise yourself starts with *knowing yourself.*

> *Fruitless is the wisdom of him*
> *who has no knowledge of himself.*
> *—Desiderius Erasmus*

Everyone in the world has good traits and bad ones. When good traits are dominant, bad ones diminish, or the other way round. It is very important on your part to know what good traits you own and what are bad.

Know yourself. Be yourself.

Avoid being weak with weaknesses, and develop being strong with strengths. Being yourself does not mean you are too superior than others, nor does it mean you are inferior than others. But be yourself, as you are. Think up good. Think up strength. Think up success. Let not the trifles, the feelings, the likes and dislikes of the people move you – to be blind to yourself. You are unique, you are special, you have purpose in life. Evaluate your strength, reform your weakness and feel great about yourself. Look at your mirror, *even if you are not handsome, not beautiful, even if you lack two, three organs, even if you have a crippled leg, even if you are with a closed eye, forever,* **still you are a human being and you can be a better human being.** Start working to know yourself, be yourself and improve yourself.

Do you know someone you like to change, regulate or improve? Fine. Why not start on yourself? That is a lot more profitable than trying to improve others.

—Dale Carnegie

Do you
decide, resolve, plan
to
improve yourself, and
build a better YOU???

You can do it for yourself

Know yourself, be yourself, evaluate your strength, your weakness and write your decision to build a better you.

My Decision

I decide_____

_____

_____

_____

_____

_____

_____

_____

_____

_____

_____

_____

_____

_____

_____

ಐ ಚ

YOU
CAN YIELD
A GREATER YOU

Is it discredit to be a dreamer? I take pride in being one........ If I did not dream dreams of India's freedom,
I would have accepted the chains of slavery
as eternal.... The progress of the world has depended on dreamers and their dreams. No dreams of exploitation and aggrandisement, of perpetuating injustice but dreams of progress, happiness for the widest masses, liberty and independence for all nations.

—Subhas Chandra Bose

Dream, Dream, Dream
Dreams transform into thoughts,
and thoughts result in action.

—Dr. A. P. J. Abdul Kalam

You too, Can Decide...

Deciding what you want most in life
is the first step towards achieving it.
—*Constance Foster*

*Y*our life is purposeful, your actions are meaningful. The moments, the hours, the years you are passing, are leading you towards a destination.

You plan for a year, for a day, even for some hours. The end result may be immediate, or may be distant, but every end depends on your choice, on your decision, on your action. The same is true for your life. You can never reach anywhere, when you are not sure to reach. The journey of life also depends on your decision and action.

Life gives – what you give to your life. When you are living for a definite plan, definite purpose, definite goal, definite dream – you are asking to get and ready to pay the price, no matter whatever the price is. *The price for success and happiness in life may be too high, but it is worth it.* Once you are determined, you can go ahead to have a dream, move ahead to fix a goal.

Dreams, desires, goals make you live a life, to experience, enjoy and realise God's plan for you.

Goals are that which induce you to strive for. Your efforts are focussed to work hard, work intelligently to reach your goal. Goals are achieved by increasing effectiveness and efficiency.

Without a dream, without a goal, life remains to be wandered, anywhere. When the destination is not known, it can lead you anywhere, without even allowing you to know where you really are. And by the time you know where you are, your life seems to be wasted! Think of your life. Think of your living.

> *Spend your life for something that will outlast it. Believe that life is worth living and your belief will help create the fact.*
> —*William James*

> *The measure of life is its excellence – not its length.*
> —*Plato*

Life is wasted when you do not achieve a worthy goal and this happens when you are purposeless, desireless, aimless. Plan your life and your life will plan for you. Ask what you want to get out of your life and your life will give, what you ask for. Most people get little because they give little to their life. Their little thoughts help them give little to their life to get little. They think they can do no better. They don't live the life really. They don't live the life enthusiastically. They think there is no chance for them.

With doubt and dismay you are smitten,
you think there is no chance for you, son?
Why, the best books haven't been written,
the best race hasn't been run.

—Berton Braley

To direct the flow, to change the course, to make a history, to invent something, to break the Olympic record, to free the people from disease, to earn or to make others earn millions, is not easy, but some people decide, opt, and act to get the most.

But most of the people do not get what they want. Because, they do not believe, and remain as wishers, not achievers. There are others who do not dare to aim, dare to dream anything, and accept whatever they get out of their life. They do not act and wait for things to happen and are satisfied with whatever is left for them.

Things change for the people – by the people, who make things happen.

- **Mahatma Gandhi,** dreamed to bring freedom for India, he could unite crores of people for a single cause! For years went for passive resistance, protested against the British rule – with non-violence and truth, finally got a free India, for you, for me, for all.

- **Martin Luther King, Jr.** brought dignity for the Black Americans – with his *"I have a dream"* march......He dreamed a nation where the Black Americans would be treated equal and judged by the content of their character and not by the colour of their skin, and finally achieved his dream.

- **Nelson Mandela** spent years in prison for a single cause, didn't deviate from his conviction at any cost, abolished apartheid, changed South Africa, and became the President, with his dream fulfilled.

They are the visionaries, the dreamers, who lived life, less for themselves, more for others, to brighten the nations they were born in.

Consider your daily life, see the things you are dependent on, look at the things you use.

The television, the vacuum cleaner, the laser, the audiotape, the cellular phone, the motorbike, the x-ray, the ECG, the contact lens....

Somebody thought of it. Somebody tried for it, somebody nourished an 'idea', developed the idea and worked hard to shape it. Right from the wheel to the satellites, there are some people who endeavoured to meet *the need and necessity, to eradicate diseases, to give comfort to everyone, everybody in this world.*

Because, they dreamed it. That is the power of a dream, to change the face of a nation, face of the world. They didn't accept whatever the circumstances were, but they thought to find something – for all. *Their hunger for knowledge, search for solution, curiosity for everything helped us to get the things that we have today.*

How do you live a life today? Are you trying to be different from others, searching for new avenues, desirous to know what is best for your life? Why don't you think something extra for yourself, for the country?

Nearly all the men at the top,
who climbed up by their own efforts,
owe their success to their ability
to do something new, something extra.
—Herbert N. Casson

You belong to this country and form the future nation. You are the future citizens, future leaders, future scientists, entrepreneurs, officers, engineers, lawyers, teachers, future people, future nation. You have the tremendous power to change what needs to be changed, what ought to be changed and make what needs to be made, what ought to be made.

Invention, discovery, progress, prosperity, happiness, success of the nation depends upon you, your friends, your contemporaries.

It is a question of your life, which in fact constitutes the life of a nation. **You are the greatest resource – human resource!** Let not the education be simply for earning – a little more or a little less, just thinking and accepting what fate brings.

I do not believe in a fate that falls on men
however they act, but I do believe in a fate
that falls on them, unless they act.
—G. K. Chesterton

Fate brings anything, when you do not act.

Act, believing in God – you will get it surely if you need it badly. You can't decide how you are going to die, but you can decide how you are going to live a life. It all starts with a purpose, with an aim, with a goal, with a dream, with a vision.

Dream Big. Aim High. Think Success. See Progress.

In the long run, people only hit what they aim at.
Therefore they ought to aim high.
—*Henry David Thoreau*

If you do not stand for something,
you will fall for everything.
—*Denis Waitley*

Think Big. Aim High. Stand for something. Dream for something. You are in the right place, at the right time, for the right action. Dream wholeheartedly, act honestly, to realise your dream. Let your talent make you a genius.

Doing easily what others find difficult is talent.
Doing what is impossible for talent is genius.
—*Henri Amiel*

We learn that many success stories today, started with dreams, at an early stage of life. They lived with their dreams – at the age you are now. That is the reason they are successful today. They had dream, they had desire, the burning desire to achieve, then – they worked hard positively. The world is proud of them, today. **The world can be proud of you too, tomorrow.**

- Today you find computers anywhere, everywhere and it does wonders! The software industry, the IT sector, changed the life of the individuals. Can you think of, can you imagine a life without computers, now? The same is true for the Microsoft to the computers. The man behind it is the richest, **William Henry Gates, (Bill Gates),** who began programming computers at the age of thirteen. In 1973, he entered Harvard University, and developed the BASIC – a programming language for the micro computer. Then, one after another, the DOS – the Windows – (the Graphic User Interface) operating system by Microsoft for Common Users throughout the world, ...Now, you know better.....

- **Dhirubhai Ambani** dreamed big thoughts to be great. He was only 16, when he crossed the borders of India. After serving in a firm in Aden, he returned to Bombay (Mumbai). Optimistically he started Reliance Commercial Corporation at the age of 25. Today, I don't need to tell you what the name 'Reliance' means to India. *Think big, Think fast, Think ahead* was the philosophy of the man who believed, who understood the mind and need of his countrymen.

- **Bruce Lee,** while he was a small child, grew up learning martial arts and acting. He worked hard, struggled hard, finally found a way to fulfil his dreams – to be the highest paid Asian actor and martial artist of all times.

- **Mohan Singh Oberoi** came from a small village. When he was a child he had lost his father. His mother taught him the power of confidence. He nourished a dream to have hotels. From a poor young man, he started his career at the front desk of the Cecil Hotel, Simla. Being sincere, diligent, honest and hard-working, he finally developed his own chain of great hotels worldwide.

- **Arnold Schwarzenegger** decided to be the greatest body-builder. He began training and persisted hard. At 18, he won his first body-building contest and the first of his five consecutive Mr. Universe titles. Moreover, he could fulfil his another dream – and became one of the highest paid movie stars in Hollywood.

- **Srinivas Ramanujam,** the great mathematician, had brilliant knowledge, during his school days. In school, all his teachers were full of praise for his quick grasp. He thought more than what he was taught and always noted down his creative ideas in a note book. At the age of 13, he solved all the difficult trigonometrical problems taught at college level. He produced new theorems of his own imagination and gave their solution. Later on, though he had to strive and struggle hard, he could reach the pinnacle of success being a mathematician of all times.

- Even as a boy of barely seven, young **George (General George Smith Patton, Jr.)** had his purpose clearly defined – to become a Brigadier General. During his childhood, he behaved like any model soldier, stood at attention and saluted his father. As he grew, he studied about Persian, Greek and Roman Generals, their battle formations, war solutions, and finally became the General of the United States Army.

There are endless examples of achievement of successful people in different walks of life, who have thought, decided, determined, to do something in life – at an early stage. They decided once and for all to advance unhurriedly in search of pearls. They knew that pebbles can be collected on the seashore, but for pearls one has to go deep into the sea....

They could have focussed on other things, they could have listened to others, they could have thought of it late...but they did not. Instead, they accepted the responsibility, dared to dream, and with devotion, sincerity, passion and hard work, could realise their dream... their goal... their aim...

When you have a sense of your own identity
and a vision of where
you want to go in your life,
you then have the basis for reaching out to the world
and going after your dreams
for a better life.

—*Stedman Graham*

You too can decide... You too can think... You too can dream...

ಐ ೧ಜ

You too, Can Dream...

Concern for man and his fate must form
the chief interest of all technical endeavour.

—*Albert Einstein*

You too can dream......
Yes, you can....

     Be responsible....

     Be concerned....

     Be sensitive....

     Be curious....

     Be creative......

*Y*ou can think something, decide something, dream something – when you feel yourself responsible. Responsibility does not stand for burden, for pressure, rather it states what you should do. Once you are responsible for your career, for your life, for your family, for your nation, you will find endless opportunities to focus upon. In your day to day life, you will find abundant instances, situations, where you can develop concern for family, concern for neighbourhood, for community and country. *Every incident will be a matter of your learning, every problem will be a matter of opportunity for you.*

- In the pre-independence era, **Sir Ronald Ross** served in the southern parts of India where, in those days, diseases like elephantiasis, yellow fever were uncontrollable. Lakhs of people used to die of malaria alone, in India. Doctor Ross had to combat malaria with all possible medical facility. He tried to investigate the cause, the reason, and thought to have the knowledge of its origin. It look him four long years, dissecting thousands and thousands of tiny mosquitoes to know and conclude that mosquito biting is the reason for malaria – which later made the prevention and treatment easier, because he was **concerned.**

  In 1902, **Sir Ronald Ross** was awarded the Nobel Prize for Medicine. Today, Malaria is 'less', still there are other diseases like dengue and chikungunya, which are 'more'.

- Pencillin was discovered when **Alexander Fleming** was **concerned** for the wounded people during World War I, and worked hard for years.

- Rayon was developed when **Bernigaud** was **concerned** for the French silk industry.

This is true for all diseases, all discoveries and inventions. Concern for difficult problems can lead you to think and act, as it is said *"Pain makes man think."* When you see others' plight, others' pain, either you complain or you think. When you are concerned, you see the problems, confusions, troubles, sufferings, inconvenience, *find and feel a need*, that is, acknowledge a need or a *necessity*. There *necessity* becomes the mother of invention, where *concern* is the father. Being concerned, you are bound to be sensitive to think, observe or perceive better. It is not essentially for diseases or for deformities but for every thing **you want to change for the better.**

It may be poverty, may be health hazard, may be space research, may be advancement in science, may be invention, you must have concern to acknowledge the need. When you get interested in the affairs and activities of your community, you think and give of your best which in turn, can broaden your horizon for thinking.

The advancement in medicine can establish a better society healthwise. Accomplishment in technical knowledge can abolish poverty or misery. Powerful solutions can be thought to control, prevent or manage natural calamities and disasters. Everywhere there is the need of thought, an idea to change, to bring a change, when you are **concerned.**

> *What do we live for? If it is not*
> *to make life less difficult for each other.*
> —*George Eliot*

Live for yourself. Live for others. Feel for yourself. Feel for others. *Getting wet is not enough, feel the rain.* Think for a good cause, stop just seeing, looking, watching, start **observing**. Observation helps to find something which exists but is obscure. Few people discover – because they observe and dare to question, what others simply see and take it easy, take for granted.

- **Newton** saw the apple falling. The question came to his mind – 'Why?' This one question later gave the law of gravitation.

- During his sea voyage to England, the deep blue colour of the Mediterranean Sea struck the mind of **C.V. Raman** and he questioned – 'Why?' And finally discovered the "Raman Effect" in 1928.
- **J. C. Bose** saw that plants did not grow in a perfect straight line and had small twists and turns. He asked – 'Why?' He later discovered that plants too have charges.

Their observations helped them to question, 'Why?' **Questions are seeds for thinking.** *He who questions nothing learns nothing.*

These could be possible because they observed, they questioned, they thought, they worked. **Newton** said: "The great teacher is enquiry."

> *I kept six honest serving men,*
> *they taught me all I know,*
> *their names are WHAT and WHY and WHEN*
> *and HOW and WHERE and WHO.*
> *—Rudyard Kipling*

The same 'What', 'Why', 'When', 'How', 'Where', and 'Who' can teach you to get brilliant ideas. As it is said, small minds discuss people, average minds discuss events, great minds discuss ideas.

Ideas give solutions. A single idea can create wealth, create employment, cure diseases, purify environment. Ideas help in development, in advancement, in invention, in discoveries.

> *Three things move the world:*
> *Ideas, plus making them work,*
> *plus making others like them.*
> *—Robert P. Crawford*

When you are curious, sincerely curious, you will find the answer or an idea. Where do you get an idea from?

Your thought, your subconscious mind taps the idea from infinite intelligence or universal power. Some say 'ideas' come from God. The great inventor **Edison** said: "Ideas come from space". Ideas come as a flash in the mind. *Dreams, goals are shaped up by those ideas......* But, do ideas come to everyone? Ideas are there for everyone, but ideas are tapped by the person who is curious for a cause, inventive for a reason. His interest activates his subconscious to tap the idea. **God helps those who help themselves.**

Everyone saw the dirty water but someone thought of the water filter. Think of the invention of the steam engine or the launching of space adventure as matter of an 'idea'. Even the key to freedom and progress is also – an idea.

> *Curiosity is one of the permanent and certain characteristics of a vigorous mind.*
> —*Samuel Johnson*

You can be a part of it, to have any idea, when you think, think sincerely, think long enough and strong enough, for a good cause. Start by an idea, end by acts. Ideas, in the form of thoughts create the fact.

Ideas can make you creative. You can see the implication of ideas from various points of view. Some of the ideas remain *inert* for some people – received, but never utilised or tested. But, some of the ideas make some people creative....... because they rearrange their variables to execute the idea.

Creativity is the struggle for improvement,
the rearrangement of variables which the human
can change in search for improvement.

—*W. W. Culp*

So develop the creativity for a greater achievement. Rearrange your variables. Rearrange your data. Rearrange your mind. You can develop the capacity and ability to execute the idea and to convert the seemingly impossible into a great success! Dream, for a seemingly impossible task which is taken for granted. Dream to do something great, something wonderful. Have concern. Dream great. Aim high – it may not be a reality today, but a possibility tomorrow. Put in your best. Have a clear vision, to fly high, to reach the stars. It doesn't matter, who you are today, what you are today or where you are today, but high aims can bring out your great mind.

High aims form high character
and grand objects bring out great minds.

—*Tyron Edwards*

Know where you are heading towards. Put your dreams in concrete form. Write them down and make each moment count.

Think progress, see success......

Do the right thing than to just do things right.

—*Peter Drucker*

To have a bright future, brilliant ideas should be conceived, nurtured, grasped. Whatever you can dream, you can do it too. Believe in the beauty of your dreams.

> *The future belongs to those who believe*
> *in the beauty of their dreams.*
> —*Eleanor Roosevelt*

There are difficult areas that need attention, difficult problems that need solutions, difficult opportunities that need observation. We have enough success stories, enough examples, enough knowledge, enough living legends we can learn from. Nothing is accidental. Nothing is a matter of luck, without effort.

> *Inventions are not accidents;*
> *they are the rewards of unceasing effort.*
> —*Thomas Alva Edison*

> *Chance favours the prepared mind.*
> —*Louis Pasteur*

Follow them, learn from them. Read about them who lived successfully and are living successfully, achieving worthy ends, inspiring people around, serving the masses, helping the poor, doing great things – all for human society, for a better life.

They have contributed their life for the country, for the world. They are our role models. We are proud of them, they inspire us, they motivate us.

Have a role model!

Keep a role model. Find who is going to be your role model, who is your source of inspiration. To dream!

Try to know him, know about him, know them, know about them, know how he succeeded, know how they succeeded....Dream high....Be bold.

Dream to be a successful scientist, to do something wonderful! Dream to be a renowned inventor to invent something useful. Dream to be a successful surgeon to do something great. Dream to be a successful technocrat to do something worthy. Dream to be a successful leader to change something for the better. Dream to exploit all the resources to advance in technology. Dream to manage disasters. Dream to feed the hungry soul.

> *The important thing in life is to have a*
> *great aim, and to possess the aptitude*
> *and the perserverance to attain it.*
> —*Johann Wolfgang Von Goethe*

Dream to have a better life, better living condition. Dream to build a **better nation, greater nation.**

The elders say, 'we are exhausted, worn out!'

The middle aged say 'close enough! settled!'

Only, you have the power to dream and fulfil,

others may simply instil.......

ॐ ॐ

You too,
Can
Achieve...

I know of no more encouraging fact,
than the unquestionable ability of man
to elevate his life by conscious endeavour.
—Henry David Thoreau

*I*t is an encouraging fact that when the dream is big enough, facts do not matter, situations do not matter, but your conscious endeavour does. It takes the same effort to aim ten feet from the ground or thirty feet high.

Never think:

   (i)   How can I think that big?

  (ii)   Who am I to think that big?

 (iii)   How can it be possible?

Rather ask yourself:

   (i)   Why it seems to be impossible?

  (ii)   What effort is needed to make it possible?

 (iii)   Whose help is needed to make it possible?

Never ask why – but develop a habit to ask **why not**?

Don't give up the possibility or probability to block your potentiality. Don't waste time. Don't procrastinate.

Don't see only obstructions. Be positive, develop expectancy and start, for one step.

The longest journey always starts with a smallest step.

Goals are building blocks for your career. Goals are dreams with deadlines. Goals are stepping stones of your dream.

(i) What is your dream for your life?

(ii) What is your dream for the next five years?

(iii) What is your goal for this year?

What you can do today –

Have your goal. Make it rewarding. Relate it to your relations. Create a burning desire to succeed, to move from one to the next, then to another, ... energising you to do better. Improve yourself. Don't think "I may not. How can I? If I fail? No, it can't be. Of course, not!" These are negative traits.

Write your goal. Find your priorities. Find what is necessary and what is not. Find what is meaningful and what is not – in your daily life, in your life.

Be sure you can achieve your dream. Don't try to do *today*, what needs to be done *tomorrow*. Don't expect great changes in a day, even in a year.

But be sure, make sure you are improving, becoming better, every moment, every day and every year and are heading towards your dream.

Think success! Believe success! Believe in your mind. Believe in your heart. See your goal. Focus on it. Visualise it. Imgine it. Accept it in your mind. See the outcome in your mind's eye.

Imagination is more important than knowledge.
—*Albert Einstein*

Imagine your goal, your dream. When thoughts are backed by belief, they remain vividly in the mind. **All things are possible, when you believe.** How can you believe? Talk to yourself, and see the outcome in your mind's eye – a positive outcome – frequently, strongly, which can create a mental picture of your success. The mental picture will pass into your subconscious mind which in turn will create your mental acceptance. You accept it mentally when your subconscious mind accepts it. When you think long enough, strong enough, visualise enough, your subconscious mind not only accepts it but accelerates you to act on your goal.

A man without imagination is like a bird without wings. Most of the people fail, even after working hard, because they think, they imagine failure. *They fail to teach their subconscious for success and listen to their subconscious for failure.* Make imagination your friend, not only for your goal but every good thing you expect in your daily life.

That is positive expectancy with belief and is sufficient enough to help you act powerfully to get astonishing changes. Break all the barriers in mind and think success! Think positive!

Your thought, your visualisation, your imagination can make good things happen for you. It can solve your problems, can improve your health, can strengthen your personality. Form pictures. Develop imagery. 'A picture is worth a thousand words.' **Talk positive. Think positive. Image positive**.

Great living starts with a picture
held in some person's imagination
of what he would like some day to be.
Florence Nightingale dreamed of being a nurse.
Edison pictured himself as an inventor.
Hold the picture of yourself long
and steadily in your mind's eye,
and you will be drawn toward it.
                                                        —*Harry E. Fosdick*

An architect plans for a skyscraper, by seeing it mentally first, then puts it on paper. An engineer prepares a plan for a dam or a bridge with the help of the mind's eye. An artist visualises his art in the mind's eye.

Imagination is the key to succeed. It creates a strong belief and motivates you. Frequent imagination directs the subconscious to accomplish, by using all your inner and outer forces.

- **Michael Jordan** – when he was in school, was not selected for the basketball team. He went home, started to dream to be good. He visualised it, imagined the ball, his actions, and accepted everything in his mind's eye. He felt he could do it. He worked hard to succeed and fulfilled one after another achievement and proved to be one of the great basketball players of all time.

All inventors, all players, all athletes, all artists, all achievers, those who have succeeded, believe in the power of imagination. They first see the positive outcome in their mind's eye – then perform the best.

Imagine your dream. Visualise your goal. Refresh it frequently.

> Refresh the picture drawn in your mind
> lest it may vanish and disappear.
> —*William James*

Imagine a day's job – before you start a day. Imagine a month's undertaking. Imagine a year's responsibility. Imagine your life-time contribution for others. Make it real, mentally, to get it real physically. It is said, *"Success is never-ending positive imagination."* Never create conflict in your imagination. Have confidence and go ahead.

If one advances confidently in the direction of his dreams, and endeavours to live the life which he has imagined, he will meet with a success unexpected, in uncommon hours.
> —*Henry David Thoreau*

By imagination, you are affirming, training, conditioning your mind to accept your goal, believe in your goal. Belief is the strongest motivator. Belief can visualise the land beyond the sea. When you don't believe, your dreams die, midway, halfway before you fulfil them.

> It is for the want of active imagination
> in their application, rather than in their
> acquisition that ideas fail. The creative
> process does not end with an idea – it only
> starts with an idea.
> —*John Arnold*

Believe that your imagination and planned effort can help you realise your goal. Break your long term goal into short, then.... shorter, shortest. *Think future, but act at present.* Give your undivided attention to the work you are doing.

> *The fool thinks everything is easy and comes*
> *in for many rude awakenings; the sluggard believes*
> *that all is impossible, and undertakes nothing;*
> *the good workman knows that great things are possible,*
> *and prudently, little by little, he accomplishes them.*
> *—A French Proverb*

Develop a habit to be positive and achieve your success little by little, bit by bit, one to next, next to next, till you achieve, in your life, for your life and for the life of the nation.

Your thought, your dream is the seed for your success. As the seed, so your dream. Your dream, must be nourished and nurtured, given water, sunlight and suitable temperature and essentially be protected from external attacks with great care, which come as fun, as ridicule to dismiss and demolish your dream.

> *Some of us let great dreams die,*
> *but others nourish and protect them,*
> *nurse them through bad days*
> *till they bring them*
> *to the sunshine and light*
> *which comes always to those*
> *who sincerely*
> *hope that their dreams will come true.*
> *—Woodrow Wilson*

Be hopeful, even in bad days and never listen to – "You can't do it! It is impossible! It can never happen to you!"

If and when, you listen to them you lose your dream..... miss your goal..... It is better...not to take it as gospel and listen to somebody, who says you can't or you are not good enough **till you try,** rather, think success and keep on trying...........

A successful man is he, who can lay firm foundation
with the bricks that others throw at him.
—*Anonymous*

Never listen to critics till you try. Be careful what they say. Weigh it, consider it, *still,* irrespective of everything they say, believe in your dream, believe in yourself, believe in God.

Pay no attention to what the critics say,
a statue has never been erected in honour of a critic.
—*Jean Sibelius*

When you listen to them, probably you may start thinking inside your heart – "I can't", "Probably it is not possible," "Probably, it will not happen to me."

Repeated suggestion, request or warning – will lead you to think, and accept them in your heart. Be aware, don't listen to negative thinkers – they don't believe in your dream, your goal, *they, in fact,* don't believe in you, don't believe in God. Turn a deaf ear *or* else give all men your ear, but listen only to your voice. Yes, your voice within. Tune it, condition it, train it for success! For achievement!

You can't fail if you resolutely determine that you will not,
because success doesn't much depend on your
surroundings as on your self-reliance.
                                                   —*Abraham Lincoln*

Never doubt! *A small leak may sink a big ship.*

Believe it. Think success. Dream big. Aim high.

You have a dream, you have a goal. Now plan to act. Dreams are fulfilled by deeds. Your thoughts create facts when you act. Your goal is fixed. Your belief is strong. Your desire is immense. Now you need to have a plan of action. Lack of planning leads to failure. *Most of the people fail not because they plan to fail, but they fail to plan.* So even for a small assignment, first plan your work and then work to your plan. Never live in hope and expectation with your arms folded. Well-ventured, well-gained. You can never have something without doing something. You will succeed when you pay the price for success.

There is no excuse. Get ready to do, whatever it takes, to live up to your dream. When the thought is positive, and the desire strong – you can build up the ability and capability. Be inspired.

You have expanded your vision. You have stretched your goal. You have denied to be satisfied with little aim. You have developed a burning desire and with a renewed mind, you need to pursue.

No other option. No other choice. No other decision. You have a changed 'you'. You have changed the stuff 'in' you to get changes 'at' you.

If not, let me ask you...

Do you think your dream is a fanciful fantasy? No. You have a dream to be someone, to be somebody, a better and greater 'you', for your family, for your community, for the country.

Build your dream with an unremitting purpose. You have chosen to be successful. You have decided *what you will go after and what you will ignore.* Your strong belief has helped you to see your dream. Go ahead, it would also help you to fulfil your dream. Go ahead, no matter what it takes to be. Never keep your dream, to be shattered. Condition your mind. Train your mind. Train yourself.

> *There is nothing training can't do.*
> *Nothing is above its reach.*
> *It can turn bad morals to good.*
> *It can destroy bad principles and recreate good ones.*
> *It can lift men to angelship.*
> —*Mark Twain*

> *Nothing is particularly hard,*
> *if you divide it into small jobs.*
> —*Henry Ford*

> *Honour and shame, from no condition rise,*
> *act well on your part, there the honour lies.*
> —*Alexander Pope*

Act well on your part. It is not enough only to have a high aim, but you have to pull the trigger.

Talk to yourself

I can't do it.	– I can do it.
It is impossible.	– It can be possible, with sufficient effort.
It can't be done.	– It can be done, if pursued.
I don't have patience.	– I can build up patience.
I may fail.	– It can be impossible, for me to fail.
It is boring.	– I can make it interesting.
I can't improve.	– I can improve.
I can't as I'm poor in every respect.	– I can, I can prove in every respect.
I can't, I am so weak.	– I can be strong.
I am simply a human being	I am a human being, God's wonderful creation.
	I can do everything with God's help.

Believe in your goal. Believe in yourself. Believe in God. Set your course, your plan of action.

> *We need to learn to set our course*
> *by the stars, and not by the lights of*
> *every passing ship.*
> —*Omar Bradley*

You can do it for yourself

1. What is your dream for your life?
2. What is your goal for this year?
3. How do you define your goal?
4. What is your plan for this month?
5. What do you do today?
6. What are your steps, to reach your goal?

In the ladder of success, what is the first step.... and what is the last?

Step 1. _____ today.

Step 2. _____ this year.

Step 3. _____ next year.

Step 4. _____ next five years.

Step 5. _____ next ten years.

Step 6. _____ next 20 years.

Step 7. To be _____ in my life.

&) C&

NOW.... START
TO
ACT

Your strong, positive thought can accelerate you to act, which can create your desired fact.

I am a dreamer, I am, indeed, a practical dreamer.
My dreams are not airy nothings. I want to
convert my dreams into realities, as far as possible.
                                                    —Mahatma Gandhi

I slept and dreamt that life was joy.
I awoke and saw that life was service.
I acted and behold, service was joy.
                                                    —Rabindra Nath Tagore

Look at the sky. We are not alone. The whole
universe is friendly to us and conspires only to
give the best to those, who dream and work.
                                                    —Dr. A. P. J. Abdul Kalam

It takes a little courage
and a little self-control,
and some grim determination
if you want to reach a goal.
It takes a deal of striving,
and a firm and stern set chin,
no matter what the battle
if you are really out to win.

                                                    —Anonymous

Be Courageous

*Courage is rightly esteemed the first of human
qualities because as has been said,
it is the quality which guarantees all others.*
—*Winston Churchill*

Courage is the quality to act, as **you** believe. Courage gives conviction to act, to do what you feel, to be right. Courage gives moral strength and helps you to start as you think and believe, thus moves you to fulfil your goal, your dream. Your belief – creates and supplies you the courage to stand firm on your decision, no matter what it takes. It is your assertive, affirmative, positive stand which can thrust away all the negative forces that might be cropping up to erode your belief by creating and instilling fear and doubt.

Being courageous doesn't indicate to be too heroic to be heedless, or too valiant to be proud, or too daring to be conscience-less. Courage without conscience is a wild beast. Be courageous, but keep your conscience alert. Being courageous means to be brave enough to accept and take responsibility, (even when smooth sailing might be an easy option) bold enough to meet the challenges and learn from it, and strong enough to persist through difficulties for the attainment, achievement and accomplishment of a worthy goal – which is chosen, opted and decided by you. Courage helps to advance in a free and fair manner encountering the negative feelings, negative talks, and insulating you from negative environment, allowing no room for excuses and alibis. Self-built, self-motivated, self-inspired courage helps you to know and realise the spiritual power that you require, and *can experience when you begin*. Your doubt, your fear may try to console in order to keep you in safe zone and can block you to lose courage, lose your dream, so that you can never make anything happen to you, which you **could** have.

> *Our doubts are traitors, and make us lose the good we often might win by fearing to attempt.*
> **—William Shakespeare**

You may commit a mistake while trying, but there is always a chance that you can correct it. You may not find the road smooth, but there is always a real prayer to sanction you the fortitude. You may be tempted to believe that you have made a wrong decision, but again it is a matter of your courageous thought to understand that it is not really so!

Never put your dream in your little corner lacking courage...

Never lose courage. Never lose the zest for living. Never go away. Live as brave men with brave hearts.

Be courageous to accept responsibility, to act

> *What would life be, if we had no*
> *courage to attempt anything?*
> —*Vincent Van Gogh*

*W*ho is responsible for your life? Of course you, obviously you! You may play hide and seek to blame others, but it is finally at your end to decide to do. Once you have decided, be courageous to act upon your responsibility. Believe that it is your responsibility for yourself, for your family, so also for your country. Your action only can ensure the fulfilment of task. There is no substitute for work, no substitute for effort. It is very easy to dream but a dream without a deed is meaningless. You can never reach high when you fear to step on.... and climb on..... step by step. Being courageous it may take a little extra, a little longer to expand your strength, nurture your stamina, enlarge your vision – to produce ideas, develop expertise, gain knowledge and experience, putting you on the way for a meaningful life.

> *Nothing was ever accomplished without effort,*
> *and nothing really worthwhile was ever*
> *accomplished without great effect.*
> —*W. George Jalan*

> *Begin not with a happy programme,*
> *but with a happy deed.*
> —*Florence Nightingale*

Sometimes when great things are thought, dreamed, decided, they seems uncertain, even hazardous. Your action starts leaving *the common mass, losing the common rush.* No great effort can be achieved easily, shortly or quickly – being safe, being comfortable and keeping always on the public road.

> *Don't forever keep on the public road, going only*
> *where others have gone. Leave the beaten path*
> *occasionally and dive into the woods. You will be*
> *certain to find something you have never seen before.*
> *One discovery will lead to another.*
> *—Alexander Graham Bell*

But it is also true that when you deviate from the common path, you are taking a chance, which nobody takes for granted easily, nobody considers it seriously, rather everyone advises you not to dream beyond your (their) grasp, think beyond your (their) reach.

The willingness you have developed, the endeavour you have planned, the effort you have started is in nobody's parameter. Thus it seems as chance! Your part is to take a well-weighed, well-measured, well-crafted chance.

> *Take a chance. All life is a chance.*
> *The man who goes furthest is generally*
> *the one who is willing to do and dare.*
>
> *—Dorothy Carnegie*

Isn't life itself a chance that one lives fulfilling his choices? Nobody tells you to jump from a fifty-foot wall, neither does anybody encourage you to jump into the sea without having knowledge of swimming. Dream to be a world renowned swimmer – but start in a swimming pool! Plan, decide and take chance today to get the result at the right time. You can't succeed if you don't try. You can't try if you fail to take chance.

When you stop trying, you can do nothing, you can have nothing, your dream may be challenging, may be difficult, may look impossible but start acting on it with belief.......with a positive mindset.

- **Franklin Roosevelt** spent much of his life in a wheel-chair after an attack of poliomyelitis, but still remained as the popular President of USA, to serve four terms of office.

- **Helen Adams Keller** was blind, deaf and dumb when she was six, but grew to author books, articles, to encourage others and became a woman of all time.

- **Kalpana Chawla** was born in 1961. After completion of her school education, she decided and joined a course in Aeronautical Engineering, and was the only girl in the class. Then she completed her Master's Degree in Aerospace Engineering in the University of Texas. Later, she fulfilled her childhood dream and became a great astronaut. We lost her.....for ever.....when the Columbia Space Shuttle met with an accident. But still....aren't we proud of her?

- **David Thomas** (Dave) was a poor orphan, even a high school drop-out, who later grew to be a multimillionaire – by establishing a chain of four thousand hotels – Wendy's International, Inc.

They are the chance takers in life – even with deformity or without, whether men or women, rich or poor. They lived their life to the best – for themselves, for others, leaving their safe zone. *Poverty, disease, hunger flourishes when capable people do nothing, think nothing, young minds dream nothing.*

Accept responsibility, take chance. Think... Dream... Decide... Start acting. Be courageous, don't develop the fear of failing before you start acting. Don't be timid and cold, nor even rude..... but Dream and be a man in the arena.

Dare Greatly!

It is not the critic who counts;
nor the man who points out how the
strong stumbled, or where the doer
of the deed could have done better.
The credit belongs to the man who is actually in
the arena; whose face is marred by dust
and sweat and blood;
who strives valiantly; who errs and comes up short,
again and again; who knows the great
enthusiasm, the great devotion, and spends
himself in a worthy cause; who at the best
knows in the end the triumphs of high achievement,
and who at the worst, if he fails, at least
fails while daring greatly; so that his place
shall never be with those cold and timid souls
who know neither victory nor defeat.

*—**Theodore Roosevelt***

Be courageous
to face obstructions

*Great accomplishments are often
attempted but occasionally reached.
What is interesting and encouraging is
that those who reach them are
usually those who missed many times before.*
—Charles R. Swindoll

*G*reat dreams are achieved surmounting numerous obstructions in the form of failure. When you have decided, dreamed and you start to act, you are sure to meet obstructions, and you can be sure to overcome them being courageous.

For every achievement there are hurdles, there are hindrances – which you need to strike away, with a positive attitude. Kites rise not *with* but *against* the wind. For great achievement, the greater the difficulties you have to face, the greater the glory you will be bestowed upon.

*The greater the difficulty, the more the glory
in surmounting it.*
—Epicurus

Obstacles sometimes stand as roadblocks inducing, arousing, instilling negative thought, negative attitude, where you may be forced to look back........ but be courageous to think success. Develop the attitude of a mountaineer..... to overcome obstacles, which may frighten you, seize you, throw you from the path of success. Be courageous. *All goes if courage goes.*

Don't get frightened. Focus your attention on the task ahead. Work on the task in hand. Find a solution.

Think of an ant. You can't stop it by putting a stone or placing a leaf in its way. It won't stop.

How did the railways become possible on the face of mountains? By going through. **Tunnels** are built. Go **through** your obstructions. Not only can you learn much more, but also you can reach your goal for sure.

It is the obstruction in the form of hardship that shapes us, refines us, enriches us, teaches us to experience good and bad, easy and difficult, common and uncommon details of our life.

Be courageous, be bold to learn from both..... even to profit out of your losses. What? **Your experience,** of course, which can enhance your knowledge.

> To a brave man, good and bad luck are like his
> left and right hand. He uses them both.
> —*St. Catherine of Siena*

Every success story is full of failing stories. Your glory doesn't lie in never falling, but lies in getting up, every time you fall. You can learn as much, even much more from your failures than from your success. Obstruction may try to defeat you. Don't forget there would be no success if the defeats didn't exist. Learn to accept defeats in a positive way, managing your mind, your emotion, forgetting the grief and rejecting the negative.

But what if I fail of my purpose here? Is it but to keep the nerves at strain, to dry one's eyes and laugh at a fall, and baffled, get up again and begin again.
—*Robert Browning*

Begin again.......take obstructions as smaller setbacks. **A bend in the road is never the end of the road,** but it is a fact you can't know, can't find till you reach near the bend. Be bold to overcome obstructions..... which arrive as unfavourable..... for your goal. Don't accept total defeat – obstacles are mental barriers, which may make you weak.

- **Edmund Hillary** conquered Mount Everest. He stated: "The biggest obstacle is to overcome the mental barrier which keeps one from trying." According to him "It was not the mountain we conquered, it was ourselves." Do you think Hillary and Norgay did not face any obstruction to reach Mount Everest? As **Hillary** says: "Hold on to your dreams, for they become realities, because we are still growing."

  Conquer your obstruction, surmount it, master it.

- **Subhas Chandra Bose (Netaji)** was the most frightening freedom fighter for the British Government. They tried to arrest him, but he bewildered them and escaped. Later he founded the **Azad Hind Fauj** to free India. Tokyo Radio broadcasted his famous speech: *"Give me the blood, I will give you freedom,"* which influenced the minds of Indian soldiers, who finally left the British Service and joined the freedom movement.

- **Robert Edwin Peary,** the discoverer, would have returned when he found the enlarged spots of water, everywhere, in place of the ice. The entire area was surrounded by it. He was with his companion Mathew Alexander Henson. At that time, Peary took out his compass to know the direction, but was astonished to see that the needle didn't move. He tried again but was shocked... because there was no other way out to know the direction. He thought he has failed in his attempt, but later he realised that he had found the North Pole, where the detector stands at 0^0.

- **Professor Christiaan Barnard,** with his team, performed the first human heart transplant in 1967, in Cape Town, South Africa. The patient lived for few days and died of lung infection. Later on more and more research in the field led to advanced methods of treating heart diseases in a better way.

There are endless courageous people, in the past, even today, doing something, creating something, building something, achieving something for a better country .... better world, facing obstructions and surmounting them. Be courageous to surmount the difficulties, remove the hindrances, dilute the obstructions – or pass through them, but never stop......

Develop a strong will.......live courageously.

What our country now wants are muscles of iron and nerves of steel, gigantic wills which nothing can resist, which can penetrate into the mysteries and the secrets of the universe and will accomplish their purpose in any fashion, even if it meant going down to the bottom of the ocean and meeting death face to face.
—*Swami Vivekananda*

Be courageous
to endure

> *No one can avoid rainfall, in a year.*
> *Into each life some rain must fall,*
> *some days must be dark and dreary*
> *—Henry W. Longfellow*

Achieving success is not easy, and the most important ingredient is patience, when courage works like the antidote for impatience, arising out of hopelessness and helplessness. *Impatience is the first reaction against a setback.* It creates an attitude of failing, unless you are courageous. Be courageous to go through ups and downs. Sometimes, you may find a curve, on the way to your goal. You may find nobody around, no source around, no help around, but remember, before every dawn, there is the darkest night. Clouds may block sunshine for a while .... but that is not the end....... Strengthen yourself to endure. Talk to yourself – you are down, not out.

> *Nothing which is worth doing is ever done*
> *without great sacrifice. Every dream in its*
> *unfolding has difficult times, times when those*
> *who work with it are discouraged, when it*
> *seems as though those who were committed*
> *to it have lost the vision.*
> *—Thomas Merton*

It may look like you have lost the vision, it may seem as if you are defeated, but it is not so. Have courage. Success is presence of mind and instance of courage in distress. An essential aspect of creativity is not to be afraid of losing. A true winner knows that losing is a part of the process of winning. **A loser stays there, where he meets the loss, but winners lose the loss, and get away from it**. No one can avoid mishaps, thus, you need to prepare to meet the rainfall and keep patience during the period of dark cloud, with a positive expectancy to get the brighter sunshine. Courage to go through misery and painful circumstances makes one more courageous. Keep patience to begin more intelligently when you feel dismayed, troubled and lose the initiative to reach your dream. Get rid of discouraging people, who are happier to see you so or insulate your mind against them. Their single word or single statement, when accepted, may weaken you. But believe in God. Don't focus more on problems..... rather on solutions. Never think of quitting, it is not a winner's trait. Don't lose your heart at defeats – that is the greatest test of courage.

Have patience. Be courageous to endure.

- **John Logie Baird** was initially an engineer, who decided to be an inventor. His early ideas failed one by one.... and made him penniless. Still he didn't lose patience and started working on 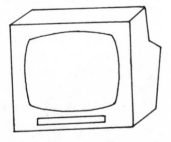 a machine to transmit pictures, along with sound. Later, he succeeded and could make the first sight and sound broadcast possible in 1931. Today, who can live a life without television?

- **Marie Curie,** (Madam Curie) worked hard during her poverty, during her adversity, patiently, for years....... in a smoke-filled room, and finally discovered radium which made her the first person to receive two Nobel Prizes, the first for physics, in 1903, and the second for chemistry in 1911.

Setbacks, obstructions, problems are sure to be encountered on the way to success, but patience, of working and waiting, gives sweeter fruit. Be courageous to endure. Energise yourself ... by saying to your inner soul that maybe the next blow will split the stone. Be courageous to endure.....

Come, courage, come and take me by the hand!
I have a long and weary way to go......
—*Clinton Scollard*

ॐ ☙

Be
Enthusiastic

*There is a real magic in enthusiasm. It spells the
difference between mediocrity and accomplishment.*
—*Norman Vincent Peale*

*E*nthusiam, we understand as great interest, great
enjoyment. What does it really mean? Enthusiasm comes
from the Greek word 'en' and 'theos' which means in
God. Be enthusiastic. Fill your life with the inspiration
from God to have power, to have burning fire within to
succeed, which comes as a strong feeling of excitement,
full of zeal, with abundant eagerness. Enthusiastic people
throw their heart completely in any work and obviously
do better. Throw your heart to any work, at any given
time, on your journey towards success, progress and
prosperity. When you strongly believe in yourself, when
you strongly motivate your 'inner you', you get
enthusiastic, your mind gets alert and it awakens you to
achieve anything, that you think and that you believe.

Enthusiasm makes your actions thrilling. It changes
your inner quality and activates you to bring out the best
in you. It takes and puts all the efforts which you can do.
Enthusiasm is the propelling force to step, to climb on the

ladder of your dream. It creates efficiency and brings out the achievements fulfilled. It drives you to do the little jobs with great care. Enthusiasm motivates your thought, elevates your attitude and activates your work – when you start being powerful, being energetic to achieve your dream. Without enthusiasm life means a mere existence full of boredom. Lack of enthusiasm makes you focus on price, rather than prize and keeps you immobile. Enthusiastic people not only work consistently, but they find their work a pleasure. **Inventors and researchers work hours together continuously..... and find pleasure in it because they are enthusiastic.**

> *Nothing great was ever achieved*
> *without enthusiasm.*
> —*Ralph Waldo Emerson*

Nothing great, nothing worthwhile was ever achieved, can ever be achieved without enthusiasm. I feel nothing considerable, nothing notable can ever be achieved without enthusiasm. If you are enthusiastic, your actions change for better. You get all the energy to get your work done. *Your enthusiasm decides your interest which further decides your concentration, your concentration decides your sustained effort which decides your work.* The more you get interested, the more you concentrate; the more you concentrate, the more you take the effort; the more your effort, the better your result. To be enthusiastic – keep your attitude positive and powerful.

Enthusiastic people do better in every aspect of life. They never make the leisure time boring, nor boring time painful, but get interested in doing something to use their time in a productive manner. To be happy, cheerful and keep their spirits high, they get interested in different activities, which matter to their life and the lives of others. Instead of chatting, gossiping, slandering, they prefer to do something worthwhile. They get interested in what they get to do, without blaming others.

Enthusiasm is a priceless constituent of your personality. It keeps you active and agile. Enthusiasm moves mountains. It can drive you, it can carry you, making you strong and filling you with physical vitality. Enthusiasm keeps you going. Enthusiasm keeps you working. It can help you to find countless possibilities, countless opportunities for you. It gets your hidden talents exposed and hidden assets exhibited. It helps you to go beyond the limit – to reach farther, reach higher. It stimulates you, it awakens you, it moves you.

When you are enthusiastic, you can overrun the obstacles, rectify the mistakes. Problems can never hold you down for long, rather you can stand against all odds to be efficient and proficient. You can find everything easy – as you get interested. You go on trying, trying, trying – because you are *enthusiastic*........

- **Henry Cavendish**, the English scientist, proved that hydrogen is the lightest of all the gases and said that it can lift objects from the Earth, as it is lighter than air. The Montgolfier brothers (Joseph and Jacques) tried and made the balloon flight possible. Later, the idea of human flight grew in the 'mind' of different people of different nations. Gliders were built for short flights.

The Wright brothers (Wilbur and Orville), who had a shop to make and sell bicycles, who did not have proper education, shared interest in this and built the first unmanned glider in 1896. They thought, they rectified, they worked hard. A series of bicycle chains were connected and propellers were made to rotate. They made the *Flyer* and finally made human flight in an aircraft possible on 17th December 1903, at Kitty Hawk, in North Carolina. Then came *Flyer 2*, *Flyer 3*, and so on.......

Several attempts, several failures, several disappointments – did not hold them back. They had enthusiasm. They thought more and more, learnt more and more, worked more and more about human flight for years and finally contributed great for global conveyance.

Enthusiasm can never allow you to take rest unless the goal is achieved.

> *A man can succeed at almost anything*
> *for which he has unlimited enthusiasm.*
> —*Charles Shwab*

Be enthusiastic. Talk to yourself, you are capable, you are efficient, think up your goal. Freshen your mind. Get interested. Get going.

☙ ❧

Be Committed

*Life without commitment
is not worth living.*
—*Abraham Joshua Heschel*

Commitment is the promise of your responsibility to perform a task, to your own self or others. It is giving **up** everything to excel and giving **in** everything to succeed. It is the determination to pursue excellence, on the way to reach your goal – no matter what it takes to be. It is sacrificing everything which may stop you from reaching your goal. Commitment is realising, accepting and determining the responsibility in a stronger sense. Commitment with commonsense does wonders. With ethics, it is greatness. Sometimes, people are committed, but they fall prey to dishonest means to achieve. Being fair, being just, being righteous – is the true signifier of commitment. In easy language, commitment means 'promise to stick to it'. You must have commitment to strive for excellence every moment, every day, to build your career, brick by brick with great care, taking every brick into account and making use of the best brick – that is at your hand, right now. You must take care of every trifle – that makes your goal, and you must avoid every trifle – that may break your goal. Commitment creates patience, develops endurance, encourages perseverance. It develops experience and instils massive faith, that strengthens you to overcome smaller to bigger difficulties and makes the determination grow stronger and greater. Obstacles, challenges, hurdles are removed when one keeps his commitment intact. Commitment restricts the 'drifting away' attitude and leaves you as 'no-other-option' person. It focusses the goal with great desire and makes returning back impossible for you. You quitting? **No way!**

Whatever be your chosen goal be committed. You can achieve it, definitely. Commitment for a cause drives one to achieve it with greater determination and greater devotion.

- German doctor **Albert Schweitzer** was committed to serve and treat people in West Africa. He believed that all life is precious and must be cared for. He served the masses and was rewarded the Nobel Peace Prize in 1952.

- Swedish inventor **Alfred Nobel** invented explosives, including the safer dynamite. But later regretted to see its misuse. He committed a fund of nine million dollars in his Will to give prizes, which we know today as Nobel Prizes.

- **Florence Nightingale** (Lady with the Lamp) was committed to serve the people. She changed the nursing profession to make it meaningful, useful and respectable.

- **Maria Montessori** was a doctor but committed to develop a unique educational program for mentally handicapped children, which later became useful for all small children.

- **Dr. B.R. Ambedkar** had strong desire and dedication to secure justice, equality and dignity for the downtrodden and deprived class. He committed to improve the quality of life for everyone, and later contributed great by providing us the Constitution. (Father of the Indian Constitution)

"Man is mortal. Everyone has to die some day or the other. But one must resolve to lay down one's life in enriching the noble ideas of self-respect and in bettering one's human life."
—*Dr. B.R. Ambedkar*

To be better in one's life, one needs to be committed.....

- Agnes Gonxha Bojaxhiu (**Mother Teresa**), a nun from Yugoslavia, arrived in India. She taught at St. Mary's High School in Calcutta (Kolkata). One day, she saw a rat nibbling at a dying woman lying in the gutter. The woman was very ill, but still alive. Mother Teresa took the woman to hospital and got her treated. Though the woman died, she moved the heart of Mother Teresa.

Mother Teresa then committed herself to look after the slum people, poor people, needy people and sick people. She treated them with great love and great care. She was awarded the Nobel Peace Prize, in 1979. She sacrificed her everything and lived a life for a worthy cause, for her commitment to God.

Commitment is the fruit of one's conviction. It is said: *"the height of your accomplishment is equal to your depth of conviction"*. If you have conviction to excel, commitment to achieve, be sure of success. Be committed – never frown, even when you are down. Get up..... get up....., because you are committed.... Step ahead, you will have power, magic to fulfil your dream.

Until one is committed, there is hesitance, the chance
to draw back, always ineflectiveness. Concerning
all acts of initiative, there is one elemental truth at
ignorance of which kills countless ideas and splendid
plans; that the moment one commits oneself, then
providence moves too. All sorts of things occur to help one
that would never have otherwise occurred. A whole stream
of events issues from the decision, raising in one's favour
all manner of unforeseen incidents and
meetings and material assistance, which no man
could have dreamed would come his way.
Whatever you can do, or dream you can do,
begin it. Boldness has genius, power,
and magic in it. Begin it now.
                                    —*Johann Wolfgang Von Goethe*

What is your commitment to God? To your country? To your community? To your family? To your own self, for your own life?

ಸಾ ಞ

Be Optimistic

*Of all the forces that make for a better world, hope is
so much indispensable. None is so much powerful as
hope – without hope men are only
half-alive, with hope they dream, think and work.*
—*Charles Sawyer*

*Hope is the companion of power,
and the mother of success, for who so hopes
strongly has within him the gift of miracles.*
—*Samuel Smiles*

Optimistic means to be hopeful and confident about the
future. Optimism is positive expectancy. It creates, it
develops a positive outlook, positive mental attitude to
expect good things to happen and finds the good in the
things that happen. An optimist only thinks and dreams,
dares and acts – to attain astonishing goals – because he
has hope, he has faith.......

*Faith is the one of the forces by which men live,
and the total absence of it means collapse.*
—*William James*

Whatever, wherever, however, progress has taken place, it is only with hope, with faith.

With hope – you dream, you think, you work. With hope you have set your goal, thought your dream. It is essential to be an optimist, to find the good in the things that happen to you. But at a times you may find yourself losing hope – even for small incidents, which you perceive as barriers. Being optimistic, you can withstand the barriers on your way and keep your hope alive. Your positive mental attitude can sustain you, to move forward with positive expectancy or else pessimism may cripple you, making you diffident, when you feel, accept and believe that you can't. An optimist converts a dream into a reality, but a pessimist converts a reality into a dream. An optimist sees an opportunity in every difficulty, but a pessimist sees a difficulty in every opportunity. People who are pessimistic never see, find or feel anything good and they expect something wrong is going to happen. They complain, even on little problems, which finally creates inferiority, insecurity and inadequacy in them and blocks their creative thought, creative energy. They find as if the world is full of bad things only and they expect, imagine, visualise all such things. They believe that neither can good things happen, nor can things ever be good. They remain hopeless and faithless.

You have a dream and you may be courageous and committed, but if you perceive only the bad, how can you advance? Every day, every moment you will encounter varied situations which might be beyond your control, so also you will come across various people who may not be favourable for you..... but still develop a positive attitude to be an optimist, to find beautiful meanings, or making the things beautiful.

We can complain because rosebush has thorns or
we can rejoice because thornbush has roses.
                                        —*Anonymous*

Two men looked through prison bars
One saw mud; and the other stars.
                                        —*F. Longbridge*

You are free to see what you want to see, but when you focus on others' faults only, you will lose your path towards progress, towards success. You have to stop blaming others, to find good, find solutions.

It is better to light a candle,
than to curse the darkness.
                                        —*Fr. James Keller*

The world is full of discouraging and encouraging situations and people. You can succeed as long as you look at the light and not the dark side. Find the light, if you really want to remove the darkness. Focus on positives with hope, with faith.

Keep your face to the sunshine
and you can't see the shadow.
                                        —*Helen Keller*

Positive people think, hope and believe, and focus on the best. When they see the cowdung, they think up planting; when they see the darkness, they think of stars to look at; when they see the rain, they think up a rainbow. They are not irritated. *They understand with every burden there is blessing and with every blessing there is burden.* They hope, they believe – to conquer, to achieve.

They live their life like a hereditary agriculturist who never expects calamity, never expects disturbances, but goes on tilling the land with hope for rain, sunshine and expects a valuable harvest. If it weren't for the hope that the sun will come again tomorrow, it would be very hard to say goodbye to it each night. But we know... we have hope... That is the essence of our life...our living.

Never get interested in the possibility of losing your goal. Use your mind as a gold mine and not as a rubbish heap – by being pessimistic. When you turn yourself absolute pessimistic, you will find the trivials as great roadblocks.

When the only tool you have is a hammer,
you tend to treat everything as if it were a nail.
—Abraham Maslow

Once, a young man met with an accident, hence lost one leg, still he thanked God – that he has not lost his life, that he has not lost both the legs, that he has met the accident, but not made the accident. That is optimistic attitude. Find goodness in even the so-called bad things, mishaps....

- **John Keats** lost his father when he was only eight years old. He lost his mother after six years. He was educating himself to be a doctor but later he decided to be a poet. It was not easily accepted by his acquaintances, relatives, but he had hope, he had faith. Keats later grew to be a great poet.

- **Charles Dickens's** father was a naval clerk who got into debt regularly and for that, one day, he was thrown into a jail. Young Charles was compelled to work in a factory and was assigned to paste labels on bottles. With hope he started writing. His early writings were neglected but he had hope, he had faith, and later grew to be a popular novelist.

- **Samuel Johnson** had opened a private school but he could not be successful, still he had hope. He began his career as a writer, then he was assigned to write a dictionary. Later he grew to be a brilliant conversationalist and a famous lexicographer.

Have hope. Have faith. Everything can be good, everything can be changed, everything can be improved.... if you think, if you hope, if you believe.....

> *Inspite of everything, I still believe*
> *"people are really good at heart."*
> —*Anne Frank*

- This quote **Anne** wrote in her diary, while she was hiding with her family, being terrified, being horrified every moment, every day, during the Second World War. Her diary *'Anne Frank's Diary'* was published after her death and became one of the bestsellers to give insight to the readers of the nightmare and the traumatic situations she faced. Read the quote again, understand her feelings, during such a state. In fact, people all over the world are really good at heart.

Even if you don't find so.... why?

What percentage? Don't be too pessimistic to consider everything too bad. Everything is possible if you believe, if I believe, if they believe – if we are good at heart.

Start from you..... they will follow.....

Have hope... Have faith... Be optimistic... Be positive...

Think the best... Believe in the best.

Think up improving yourself..... to reach your goal.

> *Count you garden by the flowers,*
> *never by the leaves that fall.*
> *Count your days by golden hours,*
> *don't remember clouds at all.*
> *Count your night by stars not shadows.*
> *Count your life by smiles, not tears –*
> *And, with this on your birthday,*
> *Count your age by friends – not years.*
>
> —*Dixie Wilson*

ဆာ ဏ

Be
Disciplined

*In reading about the lives of great men, I found that
the first victory they won was over themselves.
Self discipline, with all of them, came first.*
—Harry S. Truman

*D*iscipline is the training of mind, refining of character,
exhibition of obedience to produce self-control. Discipline
is to have self-control, to bring a condition of order and
obedience. The universe is created by our creator in a
disciplined way. Nature speaks of the discipline and order.
Life moves, plants live, animals survive – being disciplined.
For you, discipline is to be self-controlled to understand
– What needs to be done? What ought to be done? For
whom? At what time? In what way? In which place?
And how?

How can you be self-controlled, self-disciplined?

Discipline comes from wisdom – which is the result
of knowing, realising and practising commonsense. Self-
disciplined people exhibit a behaviour of order and
obedience, which is because of their untainted character.
They breathe in ethics and breathe out conscience. They never
compromise, they never sacrifice their value-based

behaviour. They never degrade their moral standard. They never shake themselves at the face of temptation, and achieve everything with fair means. **Fair means to get fair ends.**

A value-based life

Live a value-based life with dignity and honour, be self-controlled to control your senses. That is true discipline.

> *Not to have control over the senses is like sailing*
> *in a rudderless ship, bound to break to pieces*
> *on coming in contact with the very first rock.*
> *—Mahatma Gandhi*

Discipline yourself. If you feel yourself indisciplined, reform yourself. You can't achieve anything great being indisciplined. Put on a new self and never ever think of changing the output of a garbage pile by putting perfume. Let your change be long lasting. Discipline is the most important ingredient for harmonising with the orderliness of the Creator.

> *Discipline is the refining fire*
> *by which talent becomes ability.*
> *—Roy L. Smith*

Discipline is expected from a mind like you, while you grow to glow. Temperance is self-restraint in feelings, words and actions. Tongue-control is the first sign of self-control. Be disciplined to grow in talent, knowledge and wisdom. Your talent can become your ability, your ability can be your skill, your skill can be your experience, your experience can be your asset **to be what you think, what you believe to be.**

Try to be disciplined. Do the right thing, at the right time, for the right cause, for the right people, around YOU.

You can be well-disciplined, when you:

(i) <u>**Manage your time:**</u> Time is the most precious commodity on this Earth, available equally to every individual on this planet. Time can't be purchased, saved, marketed, recaptured or recycled. Make use of your time. It is going to decide what you are going to get out of life. Snatch, seize and use every minute, every moment. Be punctual – it the soul of any business.

- **Gandhiji** was a man of punctuality. In spite of such busy schedules, he managed his time well, in an orderly way.

- French Emperor **Napoleon Bonaparte** had absolute mastery over time. That is the secret of his great success.

Be punctual and manage, arrange your time, to make it fruitful for you.

> *Well-arranged time is the surest*
> *mark of a well-arranged mind.*
>
> —*Sir Isaac Pitman*

Plan for a day, for a month, for a year, for your life. Plan for the activities of the day – in the morning. Take note of your activities – in the night. Review your activities, find how much time you spent for your worthy cause! Don't surrender your precious time to insignificant chores, trifles, motions of daily life. Be sure you use the time properly, orderly, meaningfully.

(ii) <u>**Manage your relations:**</u> Manage your relationship. Respect your parents, teachers, counsellors, well-wishers, elders. Love the youngers, like your friends, express your goodwill for them. Wish them. Believe them. Trust them and let them know it. Adjust and adapt for better relationship, better environment, for a better outcome. Be attentive and try to get along.

The most important ingredient in the formula of success is knowing how to get along with people.
—*Theodore Roosevelt*

But never ever compromise with values, even if you lose your relationship. *Your life is controlled by the people, who get along with you and by the books you read for yourself.* People without honesty, slip and slide in many ways, for many causes. Shun them. Instead of extending bitterness, be in a safe zone. Greet everyone on their birthdays, compliment on their achievements. Don't be irritable, unstable. Where relation matters, ask yourself, ask your conscience, if you don't feel good. Don't treat trivialities as disasters, rather be patient, even if they seem and are so.

(iii) **Manage your life style:** Take care of yourself, your conduct, your attitude. Take care of your health, check yourself. Refine yourself.

Control yourself. Discipline yourself. Manage your life. Manage your moments.....you have the same twenty-four hours with you like the others, which is your most precious possession, and no one can take it from you. Make use of it. Fill it with discipline and power.

The way of superior man is threefold:
Virtuous — he is free from anxieties
Wise — he is free from perplexities
Bold — he is free from fear.
—*Confucius*

℘ ℘

Be Competent

Learning is not attained by chance,
it must be sought for, with ardour
and attended to, with diligence.
                                        —*Abigail Adams*

To be competent means to have the necessary skill or knowledge to do something, achieve something. Developing competence is the capacity-building procedure. Competence comes out of courage and knowledge. When one dares to learn, one dares to put his skill into action – he grows and becomes competent. *Knowledge kept in mind can never make anyone competent because of its possession.* Courage, commitment, optimism, enthusiasm – exhibited in a disciplined way makes you get motivated to develop competence, which when put into action, helps you to get the desired result of success. To be competent, you need to have the necessary skill and knowledge. Knowledge is gained by genuine pursuit, from different sources, if at all you want to gain it. Grow your **talent** to know **what** to do, and your **tact** to know **how** to do.

One who wants to know,
will always find a teacher.

—*Persian Proverb*

You must be interested in learning which alone can enhance the process of your intellectual growth, adding more and more to your knowledge bank. Learning gives you knowledge and understanding and also increases your capacity for learning day after day.

Textbook education alone is not the source of all sorts of knowledge. Degrees alone can't make you competent – though it is the chief source and vital determinant. A little extra – beyond textbook curriculum – is essential to enrich your knowledge. In spite of every possible source, EDUCATION has got great significance in acquiring knowledge for your career, for your life and stand as the **strong foundation**, to make you worth anything. It is essential to be educated, not only for scoring but for gaining knowledge. The sources and the process of accumulation and its utility can only make you really competent, to do something worthwhile. The tendency to query, the interest to understand, the effort to memorise, decides your learning pattern. You can have new knowledge when you ask new questions and allow the brain to ponder over it in order to understand and store it forever. Real reading helps to *read and think, think and understand, understand and analyse, analyse and store, store and review* – in the mind first, which can later be produced on paper for scoring, or can be used for achieving. It should be your knowledge in your storehouse of memory.

Whatever you learn, you think, you remember – it must help you to grow in your mental activity, making you intelligent, day by day:

- to perform speedy and accurate calculations.
- to understand what you read, what you hear, and to correlate it.
- to find out similarity and contrast, quickly and correctly.
- to find out the sequence of order in solving different and difficult problems.
- to use your logical strength – to understand, evaluate and conclude with your learnt, stored knowledge.
- to use the power of imagination, about the objects.
- to be able to retain and recall what is stored, learnt, experienced.

To achieve your goal, it is essential to grow to be intelligent with the power of reasoning and understanding and to be competent enough, adding knowledge from various sources, from time to time, which can help you to look for new ideas.

First of all, it is textbooks, your curriculum, your career from general education to specialisation which must be taken care of. Without a strong motivation, it may not be possible for you to learn in a better way, thus relate your advantage, your relations, your emotions to energise yourself, motivate yourself – to learn, to study. Sources you find must be used to **make, build a better you, yield a greater you.**

- **Textbooks** : Your textbook study must be for learning. It is the **primary source** of knowledge for you. Your sincere efforts alone can help you to derive knowledge and can lead you towards your goal. The teaching, the curriculum, the examination – your performance, time to time, can lift you up to step forward. Your **performance in examinations** stand as parameter of your day to day, year to year achievement, to succeed – from one step to another, completing one stage properly that fairly fulfils the prerequisite for the next, and by completing the next, you can get ready for the next. Your performance matters a lot to meet the needs of the curriculum, which ultimately decides your achievement. Be utmost sincere to your performance in studies which is the primary aspect to decide your career – by taking the help of your parents, teachers, tutors, counsellors. Studying well is very much important and you can manage yourself to study better and improve yourself, if you can lay emphasis on:

1. Know where you are and where to go.

2. Develop a study plan, managing your time.

3. Collect required materials and tools within your reach.

4. Read to learn, Read to think, Read to understand.

   (i) Read the heading – Ask yourself: What do I know about this already? Earlier?

  (ii) Read the sub-headings, paragraphs and find: How they are correlated to build the chapter? What is the order of correlation? How these relation patterns enhance your knowledge by adding new facts to old, known, stored, learnt facts.

(iii) Try to understand the chapter, paragraphs and find: What is important? What is trivial? What does it mean? What idea it gives?

(iv) Try to follow the ideas with the help of illustrations, charts, or supportive diagrams.

(v) Try to summarise mentally, to find the theme and essence of the chapter relating to the 'end of chapter' summary.

(vi) Form questions mentally, i.e. to find: What might be the probable questions according to the content?

(vii) Form answers mentally to those probable questions.

5. <u>Prepare your Notes.</u>

Notes help to study more in less time. Notes should be prepared by yourself, for yourself.

(i) As you have understood well, look again at the organisation, heading, sub-heading, main ideas, secondary ideas, important paragraphs, illustrations, charts, definitions, laws, keywords.

(ii) Establish link between them – by abbreviating, making precis and using keywords or code words or simple terms for better understanding.

(iii) Get ready for good legible handwriting, neat and clean notes – concise but not losing the essence. Go for **abc - accuracy, brevity** and **clarity**.

(iv) Present your notes in a graphic, visually stimulating way like a road map, or a skeleton or a chart – by connecting different ideas, to establish a visual pattern that is easy for memory.

(v) Prepare your notes by comparing, contrasting or supporting, proposing or in a 'cause and effect' relationship.

(vi) Outline, underline, highlight – figures, sketches, noteworthy words to draw visual attention.

(vii) Use your own keywords, code words, mnemonics, arrows, boxes, circles, in a meaningful way for better and quicker understanding.

Keep your notes for you own use and keep them in a leaf binder, for flexible use. Familiarise yourself with your notes and visualise to present your text, before you memorise the whole lot.

6. <u>Memorise, what you have learnt, what you have noted</u>.

Before you go for memorising, be sure that your brain can store anything and everything, if you are really concerned to store. Your brain has got great capacity, but it depends on you, what you store and how you store.

If properly impressed, recorded or associated, it can be easily recalled. On the other hand, when we fail to recall or retrieve, we feel as if we have forgotten. For that, it is important to store properly, which can be done better by associating new ideas to old ideas already present, and create a visual image, only to be strengthened more and more to impress better and to see in the mind's eye. Keep your old word, old idea – as keyword, to retrieve or recall correctly and quickly.

Art of memory is the art of attention.

The more you think, the more you visualise – the more it is impressed.

We remember

25% – what we read,

35% – what we hear,

50% – what we see,

60% – what we say,

75% – what we do,

90% – what we read, hear, see, say and do.

With the help of the sensory organs, the impressions become proper and strong.

This is the reason imagination or mental exercises creating visual form, sequentially or consequentially, help to remember well. Graphic notes, visual images too help us to remember well. And this is why *TV programs, cinemas are also remembered well!* Your memory power has little to do with your intelligence. Intelligence is the capacity of reasoning and understanding whereas memory is the capacity for storing.

Use it more..... make it better.

Why you fail to recall? Do you forget?

Forgetting is nothing but inability to recall, retrieve.

You forget when the impression is weak.

 - Being fully attentive, you can make strong impressions (strong reading, strong thinking).
 - Being less attentive, you make weak impressions (reading, less thinking)

  – Being inattentive, you make no impressions (reading, no thinking)

No thinking, No impression – No recall, No retrieve.

To make strong impressions:

(i) Revise – once before 24 hours, next before a week, again before one month.......

(ii) Don't allow interference of similar subjects by reading sequentially, rather allow the content of different subjects to consolidate their position in the memory.

(iii) Keep time to read and discuss what you learn.

7. <u>Concentration</u>: Whatever you do, whatever you think, it all depends on your sustained attention. *Concentration is undivided attention.* Keep the body and the mind relaxed and bring back the mind, wherever, whenever it starts wandering. Manage your internal distractions – your emotion, your thought, your physical need. Manage your external distractions – heat, light, noise, disturbances. Well-ventilated, well-lighted, well-arranged room, well-settled furniture, co-operative family members – can help you to concentrate well. Don't allow your mind to run after distractions. If you are a follower of distractions, you will definitely *find one*; if you ignore, you will *find none*.

By concentrating, you can learn better....

Learning is vital to you, for your family, for your nation. You have unlimited capacity to learn, you can know many things – new things to renew yourself, which can broaden your outlook and fill you with power to know what you can do, and how you can do.

- **<u>Books.....that tell about the Performers.....Achievers.....Successful people</u>**

There are many people who have not succeeded in life, attaining their dream, their goal. But still, there are people who have lived and are living – those who have succeeded in their respective fields. They are from small to big  performers, from big to great achievers..... in history..... so also today. You have to associate with them.....to be successful. You have to do what they do. How can you know them? How can you know about their effort?

Books...... Books are where the great men have detailed their thought, their vision, their dream and also narrated how they have fulfilled their aspirations. Read about them, know them from the pages of the books.

Learn from them. Learn from the elders.... those who have lived life. Their experience – is the store house of abundant knowledge. Knowledge about life....

Read about.....

The Leaders....... their achievements........

The Scientists..... their performances........

The Inventors.... their inventions............

Read, Read, Read – about the Explorers, Philosophers, Dramatists, Poets, all famous people in different fields.... Read Biographies..... Read Autobiographies.......

It is not enough to know *what they have achieved*, but it is essential to know *how they have achieved*. You can come across the great thinkers and their great thoughts, which can enrich your knowledge, expand your understanding.

A proverb is defined as a short sentence based on long experience. A single line, a single word can make you think – to make you useful, contributing your talent for the progress and welfare. You can get news and views of those who have lived, and who live their life successfully. You can mentally interact with them when you spend a little time, everyday, reading books.

> *Employ your time in improving yourself by other people's writings, so you shall come easily by what others have laboured hard for.*
> —*Socrates*

Books help us to recognise the true potential and bring out the best in us. It teaches about the strategies the performers adopted for achieving excellence. All the performers are, in fact life-long learners, which helps them to keep pace with progress. In the days of techno-transformation and unprecedented challenges, these slow, engaging, thought-provoking devices (books) update the self-power station for our peak performance.

Good books are the concentrated essence of the world's wisdom. Whatever is invested in a book is worth investing. When you grow, you must grow with books. When you are on a journey, when you are waiting for your dentist, when you are to relax – go through the good books which tell about the great minds.

It is said **"Books are keys to wisdom's treasure; Books are gates to lands of pleasure; Books are paths that upward lead; Books are friends, come let's read."**

- **Books for Self-improvement, Books for Self-help, Books for Mental growth, Books for Personality Development, Books for your Improvement..... Books to build you..... better and greater......**

These books are the keys to the treasure of abundant wisdom for you. These books encourage you, inspire you, motivate you. They provide calmness, patience and teach about self-discipline, self-control, self-mastery. Reading energises you to grow, to be great. It makes you cheerful and confident, even at the time of disappointments.

> *It is from books that wise men derive consolation in the troubles of life.*
> —*Victor Hugo*

These books help you to know yourself, understand yourself, evaluate yourself, grow yourself. They can stimulate you to think. To think is to live. They develop your attitude and urge you to do something great. They speak about success! Achievement! Books change the thought of the individuals. Books change the life of the individuals. Books give ideals and ideas.......Books create thoughts..... Books change lives...... Books change nations.....

> *A drop of ink may make a million think.*
> —*Lord Byron*

Read..... Read and Think...... Think and Act..... Act and Achieve......

Read books for power! Read books for success!

Read books for achievement!

Personally, I suggest you to read books, read, newspapers, read magazines, read journals.

Read good books. Gain good knowledge and put it to use. It is power......

Have moral training. Have mental training. Read holy Scriptures. Read spiritual books.

> *To be in good moral condition requires*
> *at least as much training as to be in*
> *good physical condition.*
>
> *—Jawaharlal Nehru*

Grow yourself. Glow yourself, and make your country better and greater..... by improving yourself.

You must read books ......by.......

- ❖ Napoleon Hill
- ❖ Norman Vincent Peale
- ❖ David J. Schwartz
- ❖ Claude M. Bristol
- ❖ Dale Carnegie
- ❖ Shiv Khera
- ❖ Dr. A.P.J. Abdul Kalam
- ❖ Elmer Wheeler
- ❖ Zig Ziglar
- ❖ Denis Waitley
- ❖ Robert H. Schuller
- ❖ Anthony Robbins
- ❖ Robert Greene
- ❖ Willie Jolley

- ❖ Orisson Swett Marden
- ❖ Stephen Covey
- ❖ Harry Lorayne
- ❖ Arindam Chaudhuri
- ❖ Deepak Chopra
- ❖ S.P. Sharma

Books by - all great authors.....

Learn to gain knowledge, learn to be competent. Textbooks, success stories, books for improvement, Internet, libraries, newspapers, journals are all there for your knowledge. Develop yourself. Have a strong foundation to build your dream. Your knowledge can help you to gain experience, with that you can develop your skill and your skill can be used to make you competent to achieve success and fulfil your dream....

There is a power under your control that is greater than poverty, greater than the lack of education. It is the power to take possession of your own mind and direct it to whatever ends you may desire.
                                        —*Andrew Carnegie*

Look at yourself, you have additional power of education. You have sufficient sources for gaining knowledge. Develop expertise. Be competent and give great things to the world.

৪০ ೞ

Be
Persistent

*It is a funny thing about life, if you refuse
to accept anything but the best, you'll get it.*
                                        —*Somerset Maugham*

𝒫ersistence is the continuing action to do something,
in spite of difficulties, obstructions, oppositions. It is the
action of not giving up, no way giving up, no question of
giving up. Barriers, hurdles are sure to be encountered
on the path of success – but *never give up*.

Persist. Be Persistent.

When you are committed, when you are competent
– to fulfil your dream..... be persistent...... You have your
dream, the only dream, not anything else, and you refuse
to accept any other thing but the best. Be sure you'll
get it.

Being bold, being strong, being courageous – with
hope, with faith, with love – keep on keeping on. Try, try
again is the action plan. When the goal is rewarding,
when the dream is astonishing, you will get the pull from
all corners..... but overcome it. Great things are achieved
by surmounting one after another difficulties..... only
when one persists.

When things go wrong, it is painful. Life seems dark and dull. Still smile and step forward.

It is easy enough to be pleasant
when life flows along like a song,
but the man worthwhile is the one
who will smile when everything
goes dead wrong.

—*Ella Wheeler Wilcox*

Smile, be cheerful in heart but not to create a scene of mockery. Never feel proud of your failing, but keep patience, have endurance by being happy, joyful. Many people fail because they can't persist.

An **Ant** moves......even when it is blocked.

A **Spider** works......even when interrupted.

They are small creatures with great patience. Success comes to them who persist....Persist... Harder rocks are hollowed by softer water...by persistent action (flow)! A honeybee moves from flower to flower, persistently (around 4,200 trips) to collect one single tablespoon of honey! Without persistence, engineers can't build complex structures. Without persistence, scientists can't explore mysterious facts. Without persistence, parents can't raise responsible young minds.

Persistence is the not the main thing but the only thing that matters.

Seventy-five percent of world's failures
would not have failed at all, if they had only
kept at what they were trying to do.

—*Thomas Alva Edison*

- **Thomas Alva Edison** – the great inventor, developed enough knowledge, enough experience and enough persistence to try 10,000 times! You know...... finally .....what he did, what he achieved! **Lighted the whole world ....**

- **Christopher Columbus** on his way encountered various problems, was even forced to return but still continued.....and succeeded in his exploration.

A stone cutter never feels defeated. He goes on hammering....fifty times.....perhaps sixty times.....maybe a hundred times......maybe the next blow.....next stroke.....*can split the stone ....into two*..... It is said sometimes the last key in the bunch opens the lock or.....your luck? Never be hopeless....to try....Keep on, keep on.....Never quit. It is not a winner's trait. Be courageous. When you try, try long enough, hard enough, you develop the stuff inside you....to fly.....

Pearls are a product of the oyster...through pain.....

It is said: "God's test is test of endurance"....

Have patience...... Have persistence........

> *The highest reward for man's toil is not*
> *what he gets for it,*
> *but what he becomes by it.*
>
> —*John Ruskin*

Be persistent to take over all hurdles...and no one can stop you from achieving your goal, fulfilling your dream.

How can you persist?

Persistence is the direct response of your positive thought, positive belief, absolute faith in yourself, in God.

Be confident. Be courageous. Be bold....and go on breaking all the resistance. All may say 'No' – still never give up.

All may discourage you – still never give up.

It may seem so – still never give up.

- **Walt Disney** faced many setbacks in life, still persisted and started Disneyland in California, by selling everything. It became such a great success, that after a few years, the next Disney-world could be built by spending four hundred million dollars – in Florida – which satisfies twenty million visitors every year, being the world's largest amusement resort.

- **Marie Curie** faced difficulties, yet she persisted and finally proved her greatness.

- **John Logie Baird** faced severe losses... persisted...invented television. Everyone, all those who have achieved great things are men of persistence. Finally persistence is the determinant of your success... for your dream. People who become great are the people who persist.

- **N. R. Narayana Murthy,** along with his friends, started Infosys with a little capital. They had to strive hard for years but later it grew to be great. Today, Infosys Technologies Ltd. not only technically advances the nation...but also looks after the underprivileged, the poor, by its philanthropic wing – Infosys Foundation.

Even for little accomplishments, it is persistence that pays. Years back I thought to write something for you..... but I missed. Finally one day I decided and started..... there was no favourable circumstances. Still I worked..... no congenial surroundings..... still I persisted, I went through all adverse situations.....including the loss of my beloved mother, still I persisted.....and lo! with God's grace the result is in your hands! I could give something – to inspire you, to inspire all the young minds.

Dear young minds, DREAM BIG, AIM HIGH, THINK SUCCESS, SEE PROGRESS. **Have uncommon thoughts – to get uncommon facts.**

You are **courageous**, you are **committed**, you are **enthusiastic**, you are **optimistic**, you are **disciplined**, you are **competent**....never give up. Be **persistent**, work hard, keep patience, energise yourself. Don't stop.....Don't quit.....Don't stop running....but think ....one more step..... be sure, make sure.......

You have achieved your worthy goal...your success.... your dream.....

> *May all your dreams*
> *bloom like daisies in the sun;*
> *May you always have stars in your eyes,*
> *may you not stop running*
> *until your race is won*
> *and may you always have blue skies.*
> *—Anonymous*

ജ ൯

HEARTFELT GRATITUDE TO

Abigail Adams	: Reformer, author, wife of American President John Adams.
Abraham Joshua Heschel	: American scholar, author, activist, theologian, philosopher.
Abraham Lincoln	: American President.
Albert Einstein	: German, great scientist of all times.
Alexander Graham Bell	: American, inventor of the telephone.
Alexander Pope	: English poet.
Alexander, the Great	: Ancient Greek king.
Alexis Carrel	: French surgeon, Nobel Prize winner, scientist.
Alfred Lord Tennyson	: English poet.
Anatole France	: French novelist and critic. Nobel Prize winner for literature.
Andrew Carnegie	: American steel manufacturer and one of the wealthiest man of his time, popular for his generosity.
Anne Frank	: German Jewish girl, popular for *"The Diary of Anne Frank."*
APJ Abdul Kalam	: Scientist, author, President of India.
Aristotle	: Ancient Greek writer, philospher, educator, scientist.
Benjamin Franklin	: American writer, publisher, philanthropist, scientist and statesman.
Berton Braley	: American poet.
Bertrand Russell	: British writer, philosopher, Nobel Prize winner for literature.
B.R. Ambedkar	: Politician, social activist, scholar, 'Father of the Indian Constitution.'
Buddha	: Founder of Buddhism.
Calvin Coolidge	: American President.

Cardinal John Henry Newman	:	English author, thinker, Anglican priest.
Carl Gustav Jung	:	Swiss psychiatrist and analytical psychologist.
Charles E. Merriam	:	American civic reformer, professor of political science, at the University of Chicago.
Charles Haddon Surgeon	:	British preacher, writer, reformer.
Charles R. Swindoll	:	American author, preacher.
Charles Sawyer	:	American photographer, author.
Charles Schwab	:	President of Andrew Carnegie's steel company.
Clinton Scollard	:	American poet, editor, writer.
Confucius	:	Ancient Chinese writer, philosopher.
Constance Foster	:	American author.
Dale Carnegie	:	American, pioneer in public speaking and personality development, author, popular for *"How to win Friends and Influence People"*.
David J. Schwartz	:	Professor, President of Creative Education Services. Speaker, author, popular for *"The Magic of Thinking Big"*.
Demosthenes	:	Athenian statesman, considered to be the greatest Greek orator.
Denis Waitley	:	Author, speaker, productivity consultant, (*Fortune 500 companies*).
Desderius Erasmus	:	Dutch scholar and priest.
Dixie Wilson	:	American author.
Dorothy Carnegie	:	Wife, co-author with Dale Carnegie, President of Dale Carnegie Institute of Effective Speaking and Human Relations.
Earl Nightingale	:	American author, speaker, a revolutionary for self-improvement, expert on success and what makes one successful.

Edmund Burke	: British statesman, social reformer, speaker.
Edward Everette Helle	: American writer.
Elbert Green Hubbard	: American author, speaker.
Eleanor Roosevelt	: American author, reformer, wife of American President Franklin D. Roosevelt.
Ella Wheeler Wilcox	: American, popular poetess.
Emile Coue	: French psychotherapist.
Emmet Fox	: Irish, influential author, speaker.
Epictetus	: Ancient Greek philosopher, orator.
Epicurus	: Ancient Greek philosopher, orator.
Florence Nightingale	: British founder and reformer of nursing profession, called as 'Lady with the Lamp'.
Francis Bacon	: Famous British artist.
Franz Alexander	: Hungary-born physician, psychiatrist, psychoanalyst, founder of Chicago Psychoanalytic Institute.
George B. Shaw	: Irish dramatist, playwright. Nobel Prize winner for literature.
George Eliot	: Famous English novelist, (Mary Ann Evans.)
George Washington	: First American President.
Gilbert Keith Chesterton	: Popular English author.
Grantland Rice	: American sportswriter.
Harry Emerson Fosdick	: American author, theologian.
Harry S. Truman	: American President.
Helen Keller	: American deaf and blind writer, speaker.
Henri Frederick Amiel	: Swiss philosopher and critic.
Henry Brooks Adams	: American historian, journalist, novelist.
Henry Ford	: American manufacturer of early cars, founder of Ford Motor Company.
Henry James	: American writer, brother of psychologist William James.

Henry David Thoreau	: American poet, writer, philosopher.
Henry Wadsworth Longfellow	: American poet, writer.
Herbert N. Casson	: American author.
Herbert Spencer	: British philosopher, writer.
Horace Mann	: American educator, statesman.
Jackie Deshannon	: American singer and songwriter, (Sharon Lee Myers.)
James Allen	: English author of timeless classic, *"As a Man Thinketh."*
Jean Piaget	: Swiss psychologist, professor, popular for his studies of the thought processes of children.
Jean Sibelius	: Finnish composer.
Johann Wolfgang Von Goethe	: German poet, novelist and playwright, thinker, scientist, most influential writer of modern European literature.
John Arnold	: Author.
John F. Kennedy	: American President.
John Limbo	: Author.
John Ruskin	: English author, critic on art, literature and social issues.
John Wesley	: English Evangelist, founder of the Methodist Church.
J.R.D. Tata	: Pioneering entrepreneur, industrialist, philanthropist.
Karl Augustus Meninger	: American psychiatrist, trainer and researcher in human behaviour, human mind. Chairman of Meninger Foundation.
Lord Byron	: English poet.
Lord Ed. George Bulwer-Lytton	: English novelist, playwright.
Louis Pasteur	: French scientist, discovered that bacteria cause diseases.
L.R. Kirloskar	: Indian industrialist.
Madame de Stael	: Famous French critic, novelist.

Mahatma Gandhi	: Leader, freedom fighter, the 'Father of the Nation', (India.)
Marcus Aurelius	: Great Roman emperor, philosopher.
Marcus Tullius Cicero	: Great Roman orator, statesman.
Mark Twain	: American writer, novelist.
Martin Luther	: Leader of the religious Reformation movement.
Martin Luther King, Jr	: American Civil Rights leader.
Martin Panzer	: Author, speaker.
Mary Baker Eddy	: American. Founder of the Christian Science Church.
Miguel de Cervantes	: Outstanding Spanish writer, orator.
Mother Teresa	: Christian missionary, Nobel Prize winner.
Napoleon Bonaparte	: Great French Emperor, military genius.
Napoleon Hill	: Great American author, often termed as 'Father of Success', famous for *"Think and Grow Rich"*.
Norman Cousins	: American editor, writer, speaker.
Norman Vincent Peale	: American philosopher, author, clergyman, often termed as 'Father of Positive Thinking'.
Omar Nelson Bradley	: American Army general, military leader.
Orisson Swett Marden	: Popular motivational author.
Percy Johnston	: American author, speaker.
Peter Drucker	: American author, professor, management consultant, columnist.
Plato	: Ancient Greek philosopher, educator, orator.
Rabindra Nath Tagore	: Great Indian poet, philosopher, educationist, Nobel Prize for literature.
Ralph Waldo Emerson	: Great American philosopher, essayist, poet, critic, orator.
Rene Descartes	: Great French philosopher, mathematician, scientist.

Robert Browning	: English poet, optimist.
Robert P. Crawford	: American author, speaker.
Roy L. Smith	: American author, speaker.
Rudyard Kipling	: British novelist, poet, short story writer. Nobel Prize winner.
Samuel Johnson	: British writer, scholar, lexicographer.
Samuel Smiles	: British reformer, author, speaker.
Sarvepalli Radhakrishnan	: Great Indian philosopher, statesman, President of India.
Sir Isaac Pitman	: British inventor of shorthand.
Socrates	: Greek philosopher, teacher, orator.
Somerset Maugham	: Popular British author, dramatist, critic.
St. Catherine of Siena	: Italy-born Catholic saint.
Stedman Graham	: American author, speaker, educator, management and marketing consultant. Popular for *"You Can Make It Happen"*.
Subhas Chandra Bose	: Indian nationalist, revolutionary patriot, great leader.
Swami Vivekananda	: Great Indian philosopher, reformer, orator.
Theodore Roosevelt	: American President.
Thomas Alva Edison	: Great American inventor.
Thomas Carlyle	: Scottish historian, essayist.
Thomas Fuller	: English clergyman, historian.
Thomas Jefferson	: American President, author of US Declaration of Independence. Architect, inventor, scholar.
Thomas Merton	: American priest, popular writer.
Tyron Edwards	: Author, speaker.
Victor Hugo	: Popular French author.
Vincent Van Gogh	: Famous Dutch painter, author.
Voltaire	: French author, philosopher.
Walter Dill Scott	: Scottish writer, applied psychologist.
Warren Weaver	: American scientist, mathematician.

W. George Jalan	:	Author.
William Durant	:	American philosopher, historian, writer.
William Arthur Ward	:	American scholar, author, editor, pastor.
William James	:	Popular American philosopher, psychologist.
William Shakespeare	:	Great English playwright, poet, considered to be the greatest dramatist of all times.
Winston Churchill	:	Great English statesman, Prime Minister.
Woodrow Wilson	:	American President.
Zig Ziglar	:	Author, speaker, motivational trainer (Hillary Hinton Ziglar).

ॐ ॑

*B*e happy for whatever you are today, wherever you are today, however you are today. Get ready to have massive confidence, with full of hope to live a life in a better and sweeter way.

Dr. Radhakrishnan said: You must train yourself for all-round living – individual and social. Woodrow Wilson said: Everyone should be a man of his time as well as a man of nation. John Kennedy said: The human mind is capable for inventions and ideas. Walt Disney and all great men said that your minds are the greatest natural resource. Tagore told us to keep our mind without fear and to hold the head high. Emerson said: You can't know what you can do, until you try. Aristotle said: Excellence is a matter of habit. Dr. Kalam said: To dream.... to act for a better and greater nation. The scriptures say: If you can believe, you can achieve.

Be inspired, get motivated. You have a single life to live on this planet Earth. Today's action can fruit tomorrow's destiny. Be conscious of your potential. Have faith in God. **You are born to succeed, so brighten yourself. Believe in the wonders of life and the dignity of human birth**.

Be happy. Be prosperous. Be a peace-lover. Live a life to the fullest. **Have more of you...... Build a better you......
Yield a greater you.....** Go on improving........ Excelling...... Achieving. **You Can.................**

CAN is the word of POWER

All the best!

with love,

Barendra Kumar

Mail: barendrakumar@gmail.com